monsoonbooks

LOVE ON THE ROCK

Simon Los was born in the UK. He is happily married to his beautiful Thai wife. They are now living the dream and running their own homestay resort in Thailand. Simon is also kept busy with his popular YouTube channel 'Land of Smiles Thailand'.

David Gallagher was born and raised in Ireland, but now lives in South Korea. He works as an English teacher by day and writes at night when his beloved wife and daughter are asleep. He holds a Bachelor of Arts (English Literature and Philosophy) and an M.A. in Gaelic Literature from University College Cork.

LOVE ON THE ROCKS

Simon Los & David Gallagher

monsoon

monsoonbooks

First published in 2021
by Monsoon Books Ltd
www.monsoonbooks.co.uk

No.1 The Lodge, Burrough Court,
Burrough on the Hill, Leicestershire LE14 2QS, UK

ISBN (paperback): 9781912049769
ISBN (ebook): 9781912049776

Cover design by Cover Kitchen.

A Cataloguing-in-Publication data record is available from the British
Library.

Printed and bound in Great Britain by Clays Ltd, Elcograf S.p.A.
23 22 21   1 2 3

Contents

Introduction

I worked as a bar manager in Pattaya for a little over two years in the early 2000s. My first bar was on Soi BJ. I worked there for all of six weeks before the owner attacked me with a beer bottle and I had to leave. Ironically, that owner opened up a new bar on Soi 7, and as a way of apologizing for attacking me with a bottle, he offered me a job managing the new bar. I took the job and worked there for two years.

Both of the bars were girly bars, so farangs – Thai for 'westerners' – came to meet the bargirls, and the bargirls made money off the farangs through lady drinks, bar fines, and whatever money they negotiated with the farang back in their hotel room. There was a big turnover of bargirls every month. Every month at least a couple of girls quit to go work in another bar, and then two new girls would come to replace them. Over the two years I must have worked with almost a hundred bargirls, and I must have met thousands of fellow farangs. During the day, when there weren't any customers, I often sat with the girls and they told me their stories. At night, the farang customers often opened up and told me about their experiences with Thai women. I heard about all sorts during my two years in Pattaya.

After I left Pattaya, I lived in Bangkok for a while, and now I live in semi-rural Thailand with my beautiful Thai wife. Throughout my time in Thailand, I have heard thousands of stories from people from all walks of life. Some of the stories are tragic, some have happy endings, and unfortunately at the end of some of the stories the farang ends up looking like a fool. The purpose of these stories is to entertain and to perhaps make the reader think twice if they are going to Thailand and hoping to find true love within a couple of weeks.

Some of the stories in this book have sad endings, and perhaps it looks like I am being negative about Thailand, but that simply is not true. I love Thailand. I love Thailand's rich culture and I love the warm and friendly Thai people. These are just a few of the thousands of stories I have heard over the years. Perhaps these are not the stories that show Thai women or farang men in the best of light, but they are some of the most interesting stories I have heard, and that is the sole reason for including them in this book.

Enjoy the stories, and perhaps I'll see you in Thailand one day.

Simon Los.

Sorry Sinsod

Dave, one of my old mates from the UK, used to come to Pattaya three times a year. He was a few years younger than me, but by the time I started working in Pattaya, Dave already had over a dozen trips to Pattaya under his belt. When he first started coming to Pattaya, he used to enjoy going to different bars every night and barfining different girls. But on one of his trips to Pattaya, Dave became particularly fond of a bargirl called Oh. When he went back to the UK he stayed in touch with Oh by email, and soon he was sending Oh money every month. During one quiet night in my bar, when we were having a few beers together, Dave told me an amazing story about Oh.

I hope he doesn't mind me sharing it with everyone.

Oh woke up shortly after noon. She packed an overnight bag and went out into the strong afternoon heat of Pattaya. On her way to the bus station, she stopped off at her regular noodle stall for breakfast. It was a small stall at the side of a busy road. Oh sat on one of the blue plastic chairs and watched the people pass by while she ate her noodles. She enjoyed watching people. She enjoyed watching farangs, or, to be more accurate, she enjoyed watching male farangs. After all, they were her customers. She enjoyed trying to figure out whether they were new to Thailand, whether they were wealthy or not, and whether they were looking for company. Oh had a lot of experience with farangs. Now twenty-four, Oh had already been working in bars for almost eight years. Slim, with long black hair and bright eyes, Oh never had any problem attracting farangs, but very early into her working life she realized that to make good money she needed to learn how to read farangs quickly. With the help of the older, more experienced girls around her, she learned how to manipulate farangs and pull on their heartstrings – she learned every trick in the book. Once she hooked a farang, she put all her effort into satisfying his every need, whether it be bringing him on tours around Thailand, telling him what he wanted to hear, or pleasing him in bed. She was a master at pushing the right buttons and making farangs fall in love with her.

Oh was almost finished with her noodles when she saw a fellow bargirl named Nit approach her.

'I'm so glad to see you,' Nit said to Oh. 'I need your help.'

'I'm sorry, I'm going to Bangkok to meet my parents,' Oh said. 'I don't have time.'

'Please, it will only take two minutes. Please.' Nit looked desperate. 'I need you to write an email for me.'

Most of the bargirls in Pattaya were from rural parts of Thailand or poorer neighbouring countries, like Laos and Cambodia, but Oh grew up in Bangkok. She had learned English from a young age to a good standard, so a lot of bargirls asked Oh to help them write emails to their farang boyfriends in other countries.

Nit was much older than Oh, about fourteen years older, and she was a very kind person, so Oh didn't want to refuse her. She followed Nit to a nearby PC café and read the last email from Nit's farang. It made interesting reading. Nit's farang was from England and he was due to arrive in Thailand the following week. Oh found the email interesting because the farang was asking Nit about how much he should prepare for the wedding ceremony and the sinsod, a dowry – common in Thailand, especially when farangs are involved.

'You are getting married?' Oh asked in surprise.

'Yes, next week, and then I will move to England once I get the visa,' Nit explained proudly.

Oh congratulated Nit warmly. She was glad that Nit had found a farang to marry at her relatively late age. Oh had a bus to catch, so she hurriedly wrote a reply to the email, purposefully putting in some grammar and spelling mistakes so the farang wouldn't suspect anything. When they left the PC café, Nit tried to shove two hundred baht into Oh's hand to thank her, but Oh wouldn't accept it.

By the age of twenty-four, Oh had already accumulated two million baht. She was determined to save as much money as she could and then use the money to set up a nice life for her and her family. Her dream was to own a condo in Bangkok and a house somewhere near the beach. Having grown up in the city, she loved the idea of having a second home near the water where she could escape to at the weekend. Oh freelanced around two or three bars in Pattaya; this way she could choose her own hours and not have to answer to a bar manager or mamasan (a woman who manages girls working in a bar or brothel). She worked hard for her money, but she also had six farang 'boyfriends' (four from Europe and two from Australia), who sent her money every month. They sent her money so that she wouldn't have to work in a bar and go with other farangs. They didn't know that Oh took their money every month and continued working. These farang 'boyfriends' visited Thailand a couple of times a year. If two of them happened to come at the same time, Oh would stay with the wealthier farang. She would then tell the other farang that her parents were sick so she couldn't meet. She might even ask the farang to send money to help pay the hospital fees.

Recently, Oh had been looking for even easier ways to make money. On the bus to Bangkok, she couldn't stop thinking about Nit's upcoming marriage. What an easy way to make money quickly! she thought. Oh had often heard of girls making big money from sinsods. Nit planned to move to England with her farang, but Oh did not want to leave Thailand. She had seen a lot of girls get married and move abroad with their farang husbands, but stories came back about how those girls were working in their new country and didn't have much money to send back home to their family. Oh didn't want that kind of life. She knew that people could get married in rural villages without even registering the marriage officially. This is common among Thais. Oh started to think about whether she could try a sinsod scam on one of her farangs.

Oh was an only child. Her parents were very proud of their daughter because she sent them money every month. They ran a fruit stall in Bangkok, which provided them with a very modest income. They never asked much about their daughter's line of work, but they were under the impression that she worked in the cosmetic industry. Oh had a nice time with her family in Bangkok. She brought her mom shopping for new clothes in a market, and at night she treated her mom and dad to a nice meal, but all the while she was thinking about this new sinsod idea. The next day, on her way back to Pattaya, she decided to try it. A lot of the other girls in the bars were from rural villages, so she figured she could rent a set of parents and a house from one of them for a few days. She planned to set up a farang to marry her in a village.

The following month, one of her farangs named Dave (my mate) was due to come to Thailand for two weeks. Dave was in his early thirties. He was quite well off and he had told Oh several times that he would like to marry her. As soon as Oh returned to Pattaya, she hurried to an internet café, and emailed Dave. Over the next few days she subtly suggested that she was open to marriage. Dave was over the moon and they soon started talking about arrangements in detail.

Oh told Dave about the sinsod. Fortunately for Oh, Dave was already aware that sinsods were common in Thailand. He said he would be happy to pay it. Oh said that her parents wanted a sinsod of 750,000 baht (about 20,000 euro at the time) in cash. Dave thought this was a reasonable amount. Next, Oh had to find a suitable family to rent. She asked a bargirl named Bee to help her. Bee was from a rural village in Isan in northeast Thailand. She offered to pay Bee 25,000 baht for her help, and 25,000 baht to Bee's parents to act as her parents and to use their house for a couple of days. Bee jumped at the offer; it was easy money for both her and her parents.

Oh went to the airport to meet Dave and they had a wonderful few days in Bangkok. As ever, Oh played the role of the loving, attentive girlfriend perfectly. While in Bangkok, Dave bought a nice suit for himself and a beautiful wedding dress for his bride-to-be. He prepared the 750,000 baht in cash for the sinsod and he also had to buy two baht(about thirty grams) of gold for a thousand euro to present to Oh's parents during the wedding ceremony. On the eve of the wedding they hired a minivan to take them to the small village in Isan. The next day they held a simple ceremony, with only a dozen guests who came for the free food and drink. During the ceremony Dave presented Oh's 'parents' with the sinsod and the gold. Everybody looked very happy for the new married couple. Dave didn't suspect a thing. After the ceremony, everybody drank and ate together at plastic tables and chairs that were set up at the front of the house. Dave enjoyed the party for a few hours, but when the beer ran out, he decided to go for a nap instead of going to buy more beer for himself and his guests. With Dave asleep in the house, Oh saw this as the perfect opportunity to deal with the sinsod and the gold. She gave Bee 50,000 baht to divide between her and her parents, and then she went into town. On her way to the bank, she stopped off at a jewellery store to sell her two baht of gold. Then she went to the bank to lodge all her money – almost 800,000 baht – into her account. Now she had almost three million baht in her account. She couldn't believe how well everything had gone. It was easy money. Suddenly her dream of owning a condo and a house didn't seem so far away.

That evening Oh and Dave left for their honeymoon. They got a minivan to the airport in Udon Thani and flew down south to Phuket. They spent one week of luxury on the island. Throughout the week, Dave explained to Oh that he wanted to bring her to live in the UK and that he wanted to start the visa process straight away. But first he would have to go back to the UK alone, and she would have to stay in Thailand. Dave wanted Oh to go stay with her parents while he arranged the visa, but Oh asked if she could stay in Phuket for a while. She told Dave that the weather was too hot and humid up in northern Thailand, so she would be much happier in Phuket. Dave had been surprised by the heat up in Isan, so he understood why Oh wanted to stay in Phuket. Before he left Thailand, Dave gave Oh living money for the next few months, including money to rent a room in Phuket. Oh brought Dave to Phuket airport and they both cried as Dave passed through the departure gates.

The sinsod scam worked. Oh was almost 800,000 baht up. Over the next few months, it didn't take much to finish with Dave through emails. She broke up with him after a minor argument and then stopped contacting him completely. Oh was cold and ruthless when she wanted to be.

Oh was very happy with the outcome of the sinsod scam. She started to think about when she could do it again. She had five other farang boyfriends, but she decided it would be best if she found a new farang for her next 'wedding'. Dave was a relatively young, well-off farang, but Oh knew that there weren't many young guys with that much money who would fall for it. No, she would have to go for an older farang next. Older farangs tended to have more disposable income, and they were usually easier to manipulate, especially if they had not spent much time in Thailand. Eight years working in bars had made Oh completely heartless. She didn't think about the emotional or financial affects her sinsod scam would have on her victims. All she thought about was her goal of owning a condo in Bangkok and a house by the beach.

After Dave left Thailand, Oh started working in Phuket. She had worked in Phuket several times before, so she knew a lot of bargirls and mamasans. She started freelancing in a couple of bars around Bangla road. One night she noticed that one of the bargirls, Ploy, looked very upset.

'What's wrong?' Oh asked.

'I lost my best farang today,' Ploy replied, distraught. 'This farang was the richest farang I ever met. You can't believe how much money this guy had! But today I lost him. Shit!'

Ploy folded her arms on the bar and dropped her head on them.

'What happened?' Oh asked softly.

'I don't know,' Ploy said, raising her head. 'Everything was okay in the morning but then he went to meet his friends for lunch, and when he came back to our room he said it was finished. He said he knew I had other farang boyfriends who were sending me money.'

'Maybe you can get him back,' Oh suggested.

'No, it's definitely finished,' Ploy said, and then she dropped her head on her arms again.

Oh had heard about this kind of customer with huge amounts of money before, but in her eight years working in bars she had never encountered one of them. She was intrigued. She started asking Ploy questions about this rich farang. Ploy answered all the questions. She even showed Oh pictures of him. He was an American guy named Gene. He was in his late fifties and he worked in the oil industry. Gene had only just arrived and he had two weeks left in Thailand. He was staying in a five-star hotel by the beach. Oh quickly saw the golden opportunity in Ploy's misfortune. Oh suggested that she go after Gene and then compensate Ploy if she managed to land him. Ploy agreed. She had nothing to lose; it would be like free money to her. She started to explain about Gene's habits, like how he only ate in the best restaurants and how he used to buy Ploy designer clothes and other luxury products whenever they went shopping. During his time in Thailand, Gene usually based himself in Phuket, but he enjoyed flying to Bangkok for shopping. All this was music to Oh's ears.

Oh left the bar early that night and went to check out Gene's hotel. It was a luxury hotel by the beach. Oh prowled around outside for a few minutes. She didn't go inside because she was not dressed appropriately, but there was a low wall at the front so she could see the swimming pool and bar area. Oh went back to her small room in Phuket city. She decided that to land this super rich farang, she would have to invest some money. The next day she woke up early and went to a shopping centre to buy some expensive clothes – clothes that wouldn't look out of place in a five-star hotel. She bought a couple of outfits to last her a few days. Back in her room, she got dressed in one of these elegant outfits and she packed the rest of her clothes, along with her cosmetics, a swimsuit, and other bits and pieces. Next she went to a travel agency and booked two nights in Gene's hotel. A standard room cost her 3500 baht, which was more than the monthly rent of her room in Phuket city. Oh was usually very prudent with her money, but she saw this money as an investment that could pay-off big time. The hotel was just around the corner from the travel agency, easily within walking distance (even for a bargirl), but she got a taxi because she wanted to be seen arriving in a taxi.

Oh checked into the hotel and immediately prepared to go down to the swimming pool area. With designer sunglasses, a stylish white sunhat and a book in hand, Oh blended in seamlessly to her new luxurious surroundings. It was midday, so she figured Gene would either be out shopping or relaxing by the pool. Fortunately for her, she spotted him straight away laying back on one of the pool chairs. She recognized him from Ploy's pictures. Gene looked slim in the pictures, but now Oh could see that he had a large beer belly. Also, Gene had a completely shaven head, whereas in the photos he had a small patch of thin brown hair on top. But none of this mattered to Oh. She had been with much uglier and fatter men than Gene over the years.

Oh scanned the swimming pool area quickly and decided to sit on the chair nearest Gene. She noted that he would have to pass her when he went to the bar. It was perfect. Oh got a Coke at the bar and took up her position near her target. She sipped on her cool drink slowly and started reading her book. Gene noticed this new beautiful, stylish woman, and Oh noticed that he noticed her, but she just carried on reading.

Thirty minutes passed without any progress. Oh decided to hurry things along. She stood up to go to the bathroom, but as she stood up, she purposefully dropped her book near Gene. She slowly bent down to get it, but Gene jumped off his chair to pick up the book for her. Oh took off her sunglasses to make eye contact as she accepted the book from him.

'Thank you so much,' Oh said, in perfect English. 'That was very kind of you.'

Oh placed the book next to her Coke and walked to the bathroom. That was all it took for Oh to get Gene's interest. She knew things would move quickly from here.

Shortly after Oh came back from the bathroom, Gene stood up to go to the bar.

'Would you like another drink?' he asked Oh, who was still reading her book. 'I can see you are almost finished yours.'

She lowered her sunglasses again and said 'Yes, I'd love another Coke. Thank you.'

When Gene came back with the drinks, he asked Oh if he could sit with her.

'Of course,' she said.

Oh composed herself. She knew that this would be the most important part of this project. Gene started off by asking her if she was staying in the hotel with her boyfriend or husband. He was surprised and visibly pleased to hear that she was staying in the hotel alone. He asked Oh if she was single and what line of work she was in. Oh knew these questions would come up, so she had a whole back story ready. She told Gene that her husband passed away a year ago. As for her line of work, she said that she owned a successful business in Bangkok and that she had invested a lot of money in stocks and shares. Gene lapped it up! Everything Oh said to Gene about her business and investments was deliberately vague so that he wouldn't be able to check up on any of it. Gene was blown away by this beautiful, young wealthy Thai woman. He had only ever been with bargirls in Thailand, so this was something completely new to him. Oh could see that she had Gene hooked. She decided to cut the conversation short to keep him keen. She said she had to go get some lunch, and that she hoped to meet Gene again around the hotel. As Oh stood up to leave, Gene asked if he could buy her dinner that evening. Oh hesitated, pretending to be more shy and reserved than the girls Gene was used to meeting, but eventually she agreed to meet him at the reception area at 7 pm. That evening they went to a romantic open-air restaurant by the beach. They had nice food and sipped on cocktails, with live music and the sound of crashing waves in the background. Oh really turned on the charm. She impressed Gene when she talked about how driven she was to make a success of her business. She almost had him in tears when she expressed how heartbroken she was after her late husband passed away. By the end of the evening, Gene felt like he had known Oh for months – this was one of Oh's many talents.

The next morning they met in the reception area again. Gene had invited Oh to go shopping with him. They had a quick breakfast in the hotel and then took a taxi to a shopping mall. Gene bought a pair of shoes and a cap to protect his bald head from the sun, and he bought some nice clothes and a pair of designer sunglasses for Oh. In total he spent about five hundred dollars on her. Oh noticed that he didn't even look at the price whenever he bought something. He just whipped out his card and paid for it without hesitation. Oh could see the potential for much bigger spending sprees. The problem was that shopping in Phuket was very limited. She needed to somehow get him to Bangkok for shopping on a bigger scale.

Oh and Gene spent the whole day in the shopping mall, and in the evening they went for dinner near their hotel. During the meal, Gene's face dropped when Oh said: 'I will check out of the hotel tomorrow. I need to go to Bangkok.'

'Why?'

'I have some business to take care of,' she said casually, but then she looked at him with great affection and said, 'I'm so sorry to leave you.'

'I can't believe you are leaving,' Gene said, suddenly losing his appetite. 'How long will you go for?'

'For about ten days.'

'That's when I'm due to go home. Do you really need to go tomorrow? Can't it wait?'

'I'm sorry.'

They ate the rest of their meal in silence. When they got back to the hotel, Oh wrote down her email and phone number for Gene, and she told him to contact her if he came to Bangkok. Gene looked deep in thought when Oh gave him a goodnight kiss on the cheek.

They agreed to meet for breakfast in the morning. The decision to go to Bangkok was a risky one, but Oh figured that if Gene didn't follow her to Bangkok, she could come back to Phuket after a few days and say that she dealt with her business matters quicker than expected.

Gene looked quite cheerful when he sat down with Oh for breakfast.

'I will go to Bangkok in a few days,' he told Oh.

'Really?' Oh's face lit up.

'Yes, I usually go shopping in Bangkok for a few days anyway. I'll book a hotel and flights this afternoon.'

This is too easy, Oh thought. Everything was going perfectly. Over breakfast, Oh started to think about what route to take with Gene. She could keep him as a boyfriend for a long time and get him to buy her expensive gifts and send her money every month. Or, she could try to push him towards marriage and get a large sinsod from him. Gene was far wealthier than any of her other farangs, so she knew she would be able to get a huge amount of money from him whichever route she took.

After breakfast, Oh checked out of the hotel and said goodbye to Gene. Gene promised to call her when he booked a flight to Bangkok. As soon as Oh left the hotel, she called Ploy. She met Ploy near Bangla Road and gave her five thousand baht (a little more than one hundred dollars) to thank her for her help. It wasn't a huge amount of money, but it was a couple of nights' work to Ploy. Oh had kept her word – that's important amongst bargirls.

Oh got a motorbike taxi at the end of Bangla Road. Before going to the airport, she had to stop by her room in Phuket city to pack some things for Bangkok. Unbeknownst to Oh, across the street from where she got a motorbike taxi, a farang was watching her. He jumped on a motorbike taxi and told the driver to follow Oh. The farang stopped a little down the road from where Oh got off the motorbike taxi. He watched her pay the driver and go into her room. As soon as Oh went inside, the farang took out his phone and made a call.

Oh had a quick shower and packed some clean clothes for Bangkok. After about twenty minutes, she came out of her room and was surprised to see two policemen and a farang standing in front of the entrance. She was even more surprised when she realized that the foreigner was Dave.

'This is the girl,' Dave told the police, pointing his finger furiously at Oh. 'This is the girl who took my money.'

After Oh had suddenly stopped contacting Dave he had been heartbroken at first, but his feelings soon turned to anger when he realized that Oh had tricked him. He decided to come to Thailand to track her down and get justice. When he arrived in Phuket, he went to the police and explained how Oh had cheated him out of money. The police laughed in his face. They said that Oh had done nothing wrong. Dave had willingly married Oh and agreed to pay the sinsod, and it was just unfortunate that the marriage didn't work out. The police told Dave that his only recourse was to lodge a complaint against Oh, and that way he might be able to get some of his money back. Dave got a lawyer. The first thing that the lawyer told Dave was that nothing much could be done until he found Oh. But the problem was that Dave had no way of tracking her down, so for more than a week he hung around Bangla Road from morning until late at night in the hope of spotting Oh. After nine days he was starting to lose hope, and he started to wonder if Oh had left Phuket, but then his luck came in when he saw her catching a motorbike taxi.

Oh didn't even acknowledge Dave. She only spoke with the two police officers. She pretended to be bemused by the whole situation. She insisted that she had never even seen Dave before and that she didn't know what was going on.

'This crazy farang got the wrong person,' Oh kept telling the police.

Oh and the police were talking in Thai, so Dave could not understand what they were saying. He couldn't understand why the police were talking to her so calmly. He started to get frustrated and he kept saying, 'This is the girl. She's the one who took my money.'

The police didn't know what to do. In the end, they aired on the side of caution and decided to bring Oh to the police station for further questioning. Dave followed them on a motorbike taxi.

At the police station, Dave was given time to get his lawyer and interpreter. Unfortunately they were both busy. Dave was furious. He knew that if the police let Oh go, he might not be able to track her down again. The one policeman in the station who could speak basic English asked Dave if he had a marriage certificate or any proof that Oh had taken the money from him.

'There is no marriage certificate, and I gave her the sinsod in cash,' Dave told the police officer.

'Then there is nothing we can do,' the policeman said. 'We make copy of her ID and she can go. If you bring proof next time, we can help.'

The police made a copy of Oh's ID card and let her go. Dave was fuming. He made an appointment with the lawyer for the following day to discuss the next step.

Oh got a taxi straight from the police station to the airport, and she got a slightly later flight to Bangkok than she had originally planned. Oh was relieved to have escaped the clutches of the law. She reflected on what a wise move it was to have Dave pay the sinsod in cash.

Two days later, Gene arrived in Bangkok. Oh said she was busy taking care of business matters, so they only met for a couple of hours for a late dinner by the river. But Oh said she cleared her schedule for the next day so that she could spend the whole day with Gene. The next morning they met in Siam Square, which is a shopping area in the middle of Bangkok with several shopping malls filled with high-end stores. Before they started shopping, they went for breakfast. Over their meal, Gene said to Oh, 'I really don't want to spend the rest of my holiday in Bangkok. I much prefer staying in Phuket. Can you come back to Phuket with me after a few days?'

Oh played with her food as she thought about how to respond to Gene's request. She was worried that she might run into Dave again if she went back to Phuket.

'I still have some business to take care of here in Bangkok,' Oh replied. 'Let me see what I can do. I can't promise anything.'

After breakfast, when they were walking around one of the shopping malls, Gene said to Oh, 'Your watch is pretty, but I don't recognize the brand.'

She replied, 'Yes, it's a nice watch. I've had it a long time but it's not a famous brand.'

'If you could have any watch, what watch would you buy?'

Gene asked, as they leisurely walked passed some of the most expensive stores in Bangkok.

Oh knew a bit about watches. She had some nice ones in her main home in Pattaya. She had also received some nice watches in the past as presents, only to sell them on later. When Gene asked her about her dream watch, she immediately thought about resale value.

'If I could have any watch, I guess I would have a Gucci, a Rolex or a Cartier. But nothing too bling-bling,' Oh added, because she knew that watches with a simple, classic design would be easier to sell.

Gene brought Oh into a jewellery store and the worker showed them some high-end ladies' watches. Oh pointed at a Cartier watch that she liked. It had a simple design with a beautiful champagne face and a gold strap. There were no price tags in this store.

'Do you like it?' Gene asked Oh.

'Yes, of course. It's beautiful,' she said, with pure joy in her voice.

Gene bought the watch for Oh. Gene went to pay with his card, and while one of the workers adjusted the size of the watch, Oh asked, 'How much is this watch?'

'Ninety-five thousand baht,' the worker replied. About US$3,500 at the time.

Oh thanked Gene for the watch, but she thought to herself,

I'm still not going to Phuket.

On their way out of the store, Gene stopped in front of a display of gold necklaces.

'I notice that you don't wear any other jewellery except for a watch,' Gene said.

Oh sensed another opportunity.

'I used to own a gold necklace but it was stolen. It was pulled off my neck when I was in Malaysia on a business trip,' she explained, convincingly.

Ten minutes later Oh had a two-thousand-dollar gold necklace to go with her new Cartier watch. It was a productive day for Oh.

That night Oh slept with Gene for the first time. They had a night of great passion together. Both Gene and Oh, for different reasons, were delighted at how well things were going. The next morning Oh told Gene that she would go back to Phuket with him the following day. Gene was over the moon.

Oh checked into the five-star hotel in Phuket as Gene's guest, which meant she had to provide her ID card. Oh and Gene had an amazing week in Phuket together. They spent most of their time in the hotel, and in the evening they went to romantic restaurants around the island, so there was very little chance of Oh running into Dave. As the week went on, Gene and Oh started to talk more and more about their future. Oh made Gene promise that he would come back to Thailand within three months – a promise that Gene was happy to make. Gene thought he had found himself the perfect Thai girlfriend – a beautiful, successful businesswoman with impeccable English. They both mentioned marriage once or twice over romantic dinners by the beach, but it wasn't discussed in detail.

On Gene's last day, Oh woke up early and told Gene that she had to go to a convenience store nearby to buy something. Gene had a night flight, so he was in no rush to wake up. When Oh was passing through the reception area of the hotel, she saw two policemen talking with one of the receptionists. Oh held her breath and hoped that they had not come looking for her. But then the receptionist pointed out Oh to the two policemen. The policemen approached Oh and told her that she had to come to the police station to answer questions about an important matter. Oh already knew what this was about. She couldn't believe her luck. If the police had come one day later, she would have been back in Bangkok or Pattaya, and she wouldn't have returned to Phuket for months. Oh asked the receptionist to pass on a message to Gene:

'Tell him I have to go to the police station to clear something up. It's not a serious matter and I will be back in a couple of hours.'

When Oh arrived at the police station, the police asked her to wait until the third parties arrived. She didn't need to ask who the third parties were.

After Dave watched the police let Oh go, he started to think about what evidence he could provide against her. He cursed himself for paying the sinsod in cash and for never asking for some kind of marriage certificate. But Dave and Oh had been together for over a year. He had a lot of photos of them together. He had also transferred money to her bank account in Thailand several times, so he thought that might be useful evidence too. But all the photos were at home on an external hard drive, and all records of bank transfers were at home too. Dave's lawyer confirmed that old photos and details of bank transfers would be useful evidence. Dave decided to fly home to collect as much evidence as he could. The lawyer also suggested hiring a private detective to help gather more evidence. Dave described the location of the village in which he and Oh got married, so the lawyer was confident that a private investigator would be able to find the village and talk with people who took part in the sham wedding.

The lawyer told Dave, 'If you are willing to throw a bit of money at this, the private investigator might be able to find someone in the village who can confirm it was a fake wedding all along.'

'If we get all this evidence, what are the chances of me getting my money back from Oh?' Dave asked.

'If you have old photos and bank transfers, and if we find someone from the village to own up to what happened, we will be able to nail her. But whether you can get your money back or not, depends on whether she still has it.'

Flying to and from Thailand, hiring a lawyer and an interpreter, paying a private investigator – it was getting expensive. It was easy to see how many farangs in Dave's position might give up and let the Thai woman get away with it.

Eventually Dave arrived at the police station with his lawyer and interpreter. The police explained to Oh that they had old photos that proved that she knew Dave, they had records of bank transfers that proved Dave had sent money to a bank account belonging to her, and that a private investigator had also found a woman from the village who confirmed that the wedding was a setup to get money from Dave. Oh denied everything, even in the face of all this evidence, but she was arrested for fraud.

Meanwhile, Gene had woken up in an empty hotel room. He thought it was odd that Oh had not returned from the convenience store yet. He went down to the reception area to look for her. The woman behind the reception saw Gene and explained that Oh had to go to the police station to solve some minor matter. Gene didn't think too much of it, so he got breakfast and relaxed by the pool for a few hours. By lunchtime there was still no sign of Oh. Gene started to worry. He got the name of the police station from the receptionist and grabbed a taxi. When Gene arrived at the police station, they told him that Oh was still being questioned and it could take a while. Gene decided to wait at the station, but after half an hour he started to lose patience.

'She is my girlfriend,' he told them, 'I need to know what is happening.'

The policeman who could speak English told Gene: 'Your girlfriend has been arrested on suspicion of fraud. She'll be here all day and you won't be able to see her.'

Gene couldn't believe what he was hearing. There must be some mistake, he thought. She's not that kind of girl.

Gene was desperate to help Oh.

'Does she have a lawyer?' he asked.

'No.'

'I need to talk with her to find out whether she needs a lawyer or not.' Gene explained calmly.

Some of the policemen talked amongst themselves and eventually they agreed to let Gene see Oh to talk about getting her legal representation.

When the police told Oh that Gene was waiting outside, her heart sank. She asked to speak with him in private. Gene sat across form Oh and took hold of both her hands to show his love and support.

'What's going on?' he asked, expecting to hear about some strange misunderstanding or a stroke of bad luck.

'I have done something very wrong,' Oh admitted. 'A few months ago I got married to a farang and he paid a sinsod. The marriage didn't work out so I left him and kept the sinsod money.

And then I met you and fell in love with you.'

Gene didn't say anything in response. He still held Oh's hands but he was avoiding eye contact with her.

'I don't know what to do. I'm in big trouble,' Oh continued. 'They are calling this fraud. Can you believe that? Fraud? I don't understand how this can be fraud. We got married and we broke up. This is a normal thing. Why do they call it fraud? Why did they arrest me?'

'How much money did you take?' Gene asked, cutting through her bullshit.

'Almost one million baht.'

Gene took a deep breath and then stood up from the table slowly. Looking down at a pathetic looking Oh, he said, 'You are obviously not the woman I thought you were. We are finished. I am leaving Thailand tonight and I never want to see you again.'

And just like that, Gene was gone. Oh was devastated. She had completely misread Gene. She thought he would stay by her side through all this, but he wasn't that gullible after all.

In the room next door, Dave talked to his lawyer about what would happen next. The lawyer told Dave that there was a good chance that Oh would go to prison and Dave might even be able to get most of his money back, minus the legal fees.

'Can I talk with Oh in private?' Dave asked the lawyer.

'That's the worst thing you could do right now,' he advised

Dave strongly. 'You might compromise the case if you talk with her.'

'I need to talk with her. There are some things I need to know. Can you arrange it for me?'

It was unusual, but the police agreed to allow Dave speak with Oh privately.

Oh was shocked when Dave walked in and sat across from her. The first thing she did was look around and make sure there were no surveillance cameras in the room.

'Why did you do it?' Dave asked.

'I'm so sorry, Dave,' Oh said, with a quiver in her voice and tears coming to her eyes. 'You are a good man. I'm sorry I did this to you.'

'Why did you do it, Oh?'

'I had big, big money problem. My friend tell me to do this. She said it was a quick way to get money. I had no choice. I love you, Dave, but if I no pay my debts, it make big problem for me and my family. I'm sorry, Dave.'

'Why didn't you tell me you had money problems?' Dave asked.

'I was too embarrassed,' Oh replied, wiping tears from her eyes, seeing hope.

'But we are husband and wife.'

'No, we only had a village wedding. It doesn't mean anything. If I was to marry you, Dave, I would have a big wedding and do it properly but I will never have that chance now, will I?'

'Do you still have the sinsod money and the gold?'

'No, it's all gone. I'm sorry, Dave. Don't be angry with me, please. I had big debts so I had to pay them. I still have 20,000 baht debt, but then I will be free.'

'But Oh, if I press charges, you will go to prison. You know that, right?'

'I know. I did a bad thing to you, Dave,' she said, trying to pull at his heart strings. 'I deserve to go to prison, but I had no choice. My debt is connected to my family. When I come out of prison I can start my life again, and I can be a good person again. But whatever happens, Dave, please don't be angry with me. I love you and I am so sorry for everything.'

Dave had spent a couple of hundred thousand baht flying to and from the UK, plus money for the lawyer, the interpreter and the private detective. Anger towards Oh had been building up inside him for the past few months. When he arrived at the police station, he was desperate for justice and revenge, yet here he was standing in front of Oh and his heart was melting. He went into the next room and asked the lawyer, 'How much will this cost if I drop the charges?'

The lawyer shook his head in disbelief.

'You will have to pay me and the interpreter, but you will also have to pay the police for wasting their time,' the lawyer explained. 'But why would you even think about doing that?'

'Because I still love her, and I want to help her,' Dave admitted. 'She needs me.'

Against his lawyer's advice, and to the surprise of the police, Dave dropped the charges against Oh and he paid the police for their time. Dave and Oh left the police station arm in arm and decided to give their relationship another go.

I couldn't believe it when Dave told me all this. Fortunately, he didn't ask me for my opinion about this story, because if he did, I would have told him that Gene was the smart one for walking away, and he was the fool for taking Oh back. I lost touch with Dave years ago, so I'm not sure what happened with him and Oh, but these kinds of relationships usually end badly. In truth, there are thousands of Daves in Thailand. They see what they want to see in their Thai girlfriends, and they believe what they want to believe.

It Can Eat You Up

Tim grew up in Detroit with only his father. Tim's father owned a small panel beating and painting company. In school, Tim enjoyed art, but he had no interest in his other subjects. When he was seventeen, he left school to go work for his father. Sadly, in 1980, when Tim was eighteen, his father passed away. Tim didn't have any interest in taking over the family business, so he decided to close it down and took some time to consider his next job. He eventually stumbled on a new career. He owned a motorbike and he used his talent in art to paint the petrol tank on his bike in a gothic style. Motorbike enthusiasts in the area admired Tim's work, and some of them asked Tim to paint their bikes. The more paint jobs Tim did, the better he got at it, and he started getting well known among bikers in the area. Tim lived in a trailer on a small plot of land he owned. He painted bikes in a small shed alongside his trailer.

Tim never had a girlfriend growing up. He was overweight and he wore thick glasses. To make matters worse, he lost most of his hair in his early twenties. Girls just weren't into him. Tim's life completely changed when he was twenty-four. He was knocked off his motorbike by a car. He suffered damage to his right arm and he lost all his fingers and his thumb on his right hand. Tim was right-handed so he couldn't paint anymore. He tried to paint with his left hand, but the results weren't good. Overnight he had lost his newfound passion and career. Fortunately, Tim was insured. It took three years to sort out the insurance, but eventually he received 120,000 dollars for his injuries. He was shocked to receive such a large amount. Around the time Tim received this big insurance pay out, his three closest friends were planning a trip to Thailand. A week before the trip, one of Tim's friends lost a family member so he had to pull out of the trip. The other two friends asked Tim if he would like to join them. Tim had just turned twenty-seven, he had a huge pile of money in the bank, and he was at a bit of a loose end, so he took his friends up on their offer.

Tim's friends had been to Thailand several times before, so Tim just followed their lead. They flew into Bangkok and headed straight for Pattaya. Tim loved Pattaya immediately. He loved the bright neon lights and the party atmosphere at night. He loved getting attention from girls in the bars and along the streets. In Pattaya he could live a fantasy life of sun, sea, girls, and amazing nightlife. He could forget about the monotony and uncertainty of his life back home. It was a special place, completely different to anywhere he had visited before. Tim was not a heavy drinker, but he enjoyed going to bars and finding a new girl every night. His two friends were hooked on Pattaya. They worked hard back home and saved up their money to come to Thailand twice a year. They thought now that Tim had had a taste of Pattaya, he too would want to keep going back with them. Tim spent an amazing two weeks in Pattaya, but, unlike his friends, when he got back to Detroit he wasn't in a great rush to go back to Thailand. Tim had no job, no immediate family, no prospects – he was at a crossroads in his life. His priority was sorting out his future. For the first few months after the Pattaya trip, Tim lived a very lonely and secluded life. He had nothing to get up for in the morning and nothing to help him pass away the long days in his trailer. He couldn't deal with the boredom anymore, so he decided to go on a road trip. He had always wanted to ride his bike along the west coast.

One night during his road trip, Tim visited a strip club near his motel north of LA. One of the girls working in the bar was a Thai girl named Gin. Tim bought her a drink and they started talking. Gin was a beautiful young woman with short black hair and a dragon tattoo above her left breast. She was twenty-three years old and she had already been living in America for three years. Tim told Gin about how he lost his fingers, about his old job painting motorbikes, and he even mentioned that he got a pay out for his injuries, though he didn't specify how much.

'And what is your job now?' Gin asked Tim.

'I don't have a job now,' Tim replied. 'I guess I'm still trying to figure out what I want to do.'

Gin sensed that Tim was a lost soul. Bargirls see great opportunities in lost souls.

'Don't you have a dream?' Gin asked.

'Not really. How about you?'

'My dream?' Gin looked excited to talk about her dream. 'My dream is to open a bar in my country, in Pattaya.'

'Pattaya? I've been to Pattaya. Wow! What a coincidence!'

Tim suddenly felt a connection to Gin. I'm probably the only customer you've ever met who has been to Pattaya, he thought to himself.

'You really want to open your own bar?' Tim asked.

'Sure. That's why I'm working here, to save up enough money to open a small bar of my own.'

Tim admired Gin. She had a dream and she was determined to follow it. He was also extremely attracted to her. He wondered how Gin would react if he offered her money to come back to his motel room, but he didn't proposition her because he didn't want to ruin the good feeling that they had built up together.

Tim and Gin talked together until closing time. Before he left, Tim asked Gin if he could meet her outside of the bar sometime. 'Maybe you could visit me in Detroit,' he suggested.

'My contract with this bar will finish in a couple of months. I can contact you then,' Gin replied, visibly pleased with the idea of meeting Gene again someday.

Tim gave Gin his phone number and address, and they hugged

each other goodnight.

After a month on the road, Tim had enough of travelling. He headed home and he spent the next few months lazing around his trailer again. During this time he practiced drawing with his left hand every day in the hope that his skill would steadily improve. Unfortunately, Tim was frustrated by the slow progress so he gave up again. He was desperate to find a new purpose in life.

One day when Tim was at home watching TV, a taxi stopped outside his trailer. Tim opened the door to see what was going on, and he was thrilled to see Gin step out of the car. She leapt at him and hugged him lovingly as if they were long-lost lovers.

'What are you doing here?' Tim asked, still hugging her.

'My contract in the bar finished a few days ago, so I came straight here to meet you. I missed you.'

Gin moved into the trailer with Tim, and within twenty-four hours they were officially a couple. Tim showed his new girlfriend around Detroit some days, but on other days they just hung around the trailer and enjoyed each other's company. A month passed like this, and then one day Gin told Tim that it was time for her to move back to Thailand and start looking for a bar. Gin looked closely at Tim to see how he took the news. As she expected, Tim was devastated to hear that she was leaving him.

'Why don't you come with me?' Gin suggested, acting like the idea had just occurred to her. 'We can open the bar together. What do you think?'

Tim took a few days to think about Gin's appealing offer, but in the end he turned her down.

'I don't know enough about Thailand,' Tim explained. 'I would like to go back there again someday because it's a lovely country, but I'm not ready to leave America and start a new life in Thailand.'

Gin was annoyed at Tim for a few days, but she knew better than to burn her bridges. She made up with Tim and they spent one last week together as a loving couple before Gin flew back to Thailand.

Tim and Gin called each other a few times during the first few months, but they soon lost contact completely. Soon after Gin left, Tim started working again. His friend (the friend who had pulled out of the Thailand trip) owned three restaurants, and he offered Tim a job as a cashier in one of them. Tim was content living alone and doing a simple job. He didn't have any stress or worries in his life, and of course he was financially secure. He had a comfortable life, but there wasn't much joy or pleasure in it. Ten years rolled by like this, and then in the first week of the year 2000, when Tim was 37, he got a call out of the blue from Gin. He was gobsmacked!

'Happy new year!' she said, as if they had just spoken last week. 'How have you been? Any news?'

Tim felt a little embarrassed because his life had hardly changed since he had last met Gin. He told her about his job in the restaurant, but apart from that he didn't have much news to share. Tim was dying to hear what Gin had been doing for the past ten years.

'Did you open your bar in Pattaya?' Tim asked.

'You remember! Yes, I opened my bar in Pattaya,' Gin replied. 'But now I no have.'

'Why? What happened?'

'My family had a problem last year,' Gin said, suddenly sounding very sad. 'I had to go home to take care of my family. I lose money and bar, but no problem. Maybe I will open a new bar this year. I miss you.'

Tim and Gin called each other a couple of times a week for the next month. At first they mostly talked about the time they had shared together in Detroit, but then they started to talk about the future they hoped to have together. One day Gin asked Tim directly: 'Why don't you come to live in Thailand? We can run a business together.'

Tim was single and he was living a desperately lonely life. Nothing had worked out for him in America. He was stuck in a rut. There was a beautiful girl on the other side of the world who wanted to be his girlfriend, and he had money in the bank, so he decided it was time for a new start. He sold his land, trailer and bike for about twenty thousand dollars, he worked out his notice at the restaurant, and then off he flew to Thailand to start his new life.

Tim hoped that he would have more luck in Thailand than he did back in America. He was excited about this adventure. He looked forward to living in a beautiful country and starting up a new business with Gin. When he was in Pattaya all those years ago, he had seen a lot of farangs running their own bars, so he figured there must be money in it. But Tim still knew very little about Thailand. He didn't know about the local customs or laws, nor did he know how much it would cost to set up and run a bar.

Tim flew into Bangkok and got a taxi to Pattaya. The taxi dropped him off on Beach road. He didn't have a hotel booked, so he walked up and down a couple of streets until he found a hotel with a pool for eight hundred baht a night. As soon as he checked in, he called Gin from the hotel phone and told her which hotel he was staying in. Fifteen minutes later, she arrived at the hotel. Gin brought Tim to a nice pizza and pasta restaurant by the beach, and while they were eating she started talking business.

'I have been looking at some bars,' she said. 'Now is a good time, a very good time, to get a bar. Tomorrow ...'

Tim stopped her mid-sentence. 'Gin, I'm sorry, but I just arrived in Thailand. I need some time to settle in first. I don't know anything about Thailand or about business in Thailand yet. Let's not talk about business for a while. I need time.'

'While you are getting used to Thailand, we can just go look at some bars. There's no harm in just looking,' Gin suggested.

'But I don't even know if I want to run a bar. I know nothing about bars. I was thinking it might be better to open a tattoo store. I can practice drawing with my left hand more, or I can hire a good tattooist.'

Gin didn't push the matter. She knew that she had Tim hooked, but she realized that he wasn't ready to commit to a business yet. So, she resorted to plan B. She suggested renting a motorbike and driving all around Pattaya for the next month, and of course Gin planned to use this time to show Tim different kinds of bars and locations.

Tim really enjoyed his first two months in Pattaya. During the day, Tim and Gin relaxed by the pool or the beach, and in the evening, when the weather was cooler, they got on their bike and went off exploring Pattaya. Tim started to love his new city.

Gin had her heart set on getting a new bar, but she knew from past experience that a new bar would be expensive to set up. She would have to pay key money up front, which is the equivalent of one year's rent, and monthly rent on top of that. She didn't have that kind of money after her last bar failed. That's why she needed Tim. But Tim was not sold on the idea of opening a bar. He was leaning more towards opening a tattoo store, so during his first two months in Pattaya he visited several tattoo stores in the area and inquired about what it would take to set up a store of his own. The more information he got, the more he realized how much he had to learn. He eventually gave up on the idea of opening a tattoo store because he didn't know anything about the needles, the machinery or the hygiene involved. Now that the tattoo store idea was off the table, Tim didn't have many options left. He didn't really have enough money to make a go of a guesthouse or a hotel. He struggled to make a decision about his future. The only thing Tim was sure of was that he didn't want to go back to America; he wanted to stay in Thailand with Gin. Finally, he told Gin, 'Let's find a bar that's not expensive, but that we can make a living off of. We can start small and maybe build on it later.'

'My friends told me about four bars that are available,' Gin said, delighted that Tim had finally come around to her way of thinking. 'Let's have a look at them tomorrow.'

Out of the four bars they went to see, one bar really stood out. It was a small bar on Soi 8, a couple of doors down from Sailor Bar towards the beach. This bar was run by a farang and his girlfriend, but they had recently broken up. They were three months into their second year, but the farang had had enough of the bar and wanted out. Tim got a great deal. He agreed to take over the bar with all the stock, a big TV and everything else in place to open the bar straight away. The only downside was that the landlord could only give them a lease for the rest of the year and one more year on top of that. The monthly rent was steep at twenty thousand baht, but at the time Soi 8 was the busiest place in Pattaya, apart from Walking Street. Before signing anything, Tim and Gin said they wanted to work in the bar for a week to see if there were any problems. The farang said he would not be in the bar that week, but he agreed to let Tim and Gin work and observe the business. Tim and Gin went to the bar every day for a week, but they didn't stay there from opening time to closing time. Instead, they went to the bar for a couple of hours at night when the bar was at its busiest. Gin did this on purpose. She wanted Tim to see the bar when it was full of customers and taking in a lot of money. She was worried that Tim might get cold feet and pull out before they signed the lease if he saw the bar in the early evening when the place was dead. Tim was happy with what he saw throughout the week. He transferred ten thousand dollars from his American bank account to cover all the costs. They never even discussed using Gin's money.

Tim and Gin closed the bar for a week. They spent about a thousand dollars on changing the bar's name and some of its decor. Most of the other bars had several girls outside the bars dragging customers in off the streets, but Gin knew that if she hired a lot of girls, she would have a lot of salaries to pay at the end of the month. She had made that mistake in her last bar, so this time she wanted to start-off small. She found a few freelancers to work in the bar, and they brought some of their friends to work too. They opened the bar at the start of high season, so there were plenty of customers every night. Gin assumed the role of cashier. Tim didn't have a work permit, so he was never allowed to go behind the bar. He sat at the bar every night and played the role of the friendly, welcoming host. This was common for farang bar managers at the time.

The first four months went great. They had to pay the girls for each lady drink and a percentage of each bar fine, but they were making enough money to cover all their expenses (including their bike rental and Tim's hotel room), and they even managed to save some money in the bank each month. There was a great buzz around Soi 8 at that time. Guys loved walking up and down Soi 8 because of all the attention they got from girls standing outside the bars, trying to drag them inside. It was teeming with people every night during high season. Every bar was making money. Tim was enjoying his new life. His bar was successful and he was getting on well with Gin.

I met Tim for the first time as high season was coming to a close. I was running a bar on Soi 7, around the back of Tim's bar. One night I was walking down Soi 8 after playing in a snooker competition, and I thought I would stop in at Tim's bar for a drink. Tim and I started chatting and we really hit it off. He was a very friendly and easygoing guy. He didn't drink much, and I remember thinking that that was unusual for a farang bar manager in Pattaya. Over the next month we became friends. Sometimes he visited my bar, and other times I popped into his bar for a drink. When low season came, there was a huge drop off in customers. The constant stream of customers that walked up and down Soi 8 every night suddenly disappeared. Tim came to my bar one afternoon to tell me about his concerns.

'We have been making a loss for the last few weeks,' he said to me. 'Our bar used to be full every night. Where have all the customers gone?'

Tim had not prepared himself for low season.

'Our bar is barely breaking even,' I told him. 'Most bars only break even or make a slight loss during low season, and then they make their real money during high season. My advice to you would be to keep your costs down as much as you can during low season. You'd save yourself a lot of money if you moved out of that hotel and found an apartment.'

He followed my advice, and with the help of Gin he found an apartment on the third road in from the beach. The apartment was a bit dark and gloomy, but there was a swimming pool in the complex and the rent was only 3,500 baht a month. Tim also thought he was wasting money by renting a bike, so he thought it would make sense to buy a bike of his own. He bought a new Honda Wave.

Tim loved his new bike. He bought it for about a thousand dollars, and he spent a further two thousand dollars customizing it. It was crazy! He had coloured nuts and bolts put into the bike, he upgraded the chain guard and his seat, he customized the lights, and he customized the exhaust pipe to make it much louder. He also paid a guy to paint the petrol tank in a gothic style, just like his old bike back in Detroit. I couldn't understand how he could go from being so concerned about making a slight loss in his bar one month to splashing all that money customizing his bike the next month. It made no sense to me, but it was Tim's passion. Plus, it was a talking point; if you saw this unique bike at the end of Soi 8, you knew that Tim was in his bar.

I started noticing a change in Tim about two months into low season. He started drinking more. During low season he never gave a drink to a customer on the house, and he never refused a drink from a customer. He saw these free drinks as a kind of earnings, so he took as much as he could. When I first met Tim, he was a friendly warm-hearted guy, but the stress of low season and his new drinking habit had hardened him up and made him into a scrooge. He wasn't only drinking beer anymore either; he usually moved onto whiskey and other shorts towards the end of the night, and this took its toll. For the first time in their relationship, arguments started to pop up between Tim and Gin. These arguments were often played out in the bar for all to see, so that couldn't have been good for business.

Tim and Gin's apartment really was dark and depressing. They decided to find a nicer and brighter place to live. They found a two-bedroom bungalow a couple of kilometres outside of the downtown area, on the other side of Sukhumvit Road. The bungalow didn't have a pool and it was expensive at 15,000 baht a month, but it was bright and spacious. As soon as they moved into their new home, both Tim and Gin looked much happier. Tim seemed to stop worrying about the lack of customers. He finally grasped the idea that making a slight loss during low season is par for the course.

When high season came around again, the customers came flooding back and Tim was drinking more than ever. He had also gotten a taste for the local white whiskey – Lao Khao – which is a cheap and nasty drink that most farangs stay away from. Tim's bar was busy every night, and a lot of customers offered to buy Tim a drink. He kept his policy of never refusing a drink. He was getting hammered every night. The bar was making plenty of money again so Gin didn't really care that Tim was drinking too much. Plus, they didn't fight anymore because Tim was always either drunk on his stool at the end of the bar or asleep back in the bungalow. Everything was going well except for Tim's drinking habit.

Before they knew it, high season came to an end and low season reared its ugly head again. Tim kept drinking and I noticed that he started drinking earlier in the evening as low season went on. A lot of bar managers in Pattaya, including myself, used to drink a lot, but the Lao Khao was really making Tim blind drunk every night. I was worried about Tim, so one day I visited his bar to express my concerns. We actually had a bit of a falling out over it because he told me he was fine and that I should mind my own business. After that, I still popped in to his bar every now and then to say hello, but he kind of pushed me away because of his drinking habit. Tim was a mess. Gin, on the other hand, carried on with her life – business as usual. She was working, sleeping and putting money in the bank. Everything was going well as far as she was concerned.

One day I was walking down Soi 8 shortly after lunch and I saw Tim sitting in his bar alone. I was surprised to see him at this time because usually he arrived at the bar in the evening. I was also surprised that he was sober and drinking a cup of coffee. Tim had not been very friendly towards me since I confronted him about his drinking, but this time he was fine with me. We made small talk for a few minutes and then out of the blue he broke down in tears in front of me.

'I'm fed up, Simon,' he cried. 'I'm fed up with Gin, I'm fed up with this bar, I'm fed up with everything!'

I patted him on the back until he calmed down.

'Maybe running a bar is not the best thing for you,' I told him. 'Maybe you should start drawing again and maybe try to get into tattooing.'

'A lot of other people have told me the same thing,' he said.

He seemed to take my advice on board and he thanked me for being a good friend.

A week or two passed – you lose track of time in Pattaya. I was walking down Soi 8 one night and I saw Tim asleep at the bar. He had obviously been drinking. There were no customers, and Gin and two freelancers were laughing and joking with each other at the front of the bar. I never saw it for myself, but several people told me at the time that Tim had started to lose his cool and shout at customers quite often. As a bar manager, you just cannot do that because you are relying on those customers to pay your bills. Tim was going down a slippery slope. It was hard to watch. To make matters worse, low season was particularly quiet that year. A lot of bar owners were closing up and walking away. When Tim's lease was coming to an end, I thought he might pack it in and move onto something new, but he decided to stick with it. It cost him extra money, but Tim signed a lease for another year.

Songkran is a water festival that marks the start of the traditional Thai New Year. Thai people celebrate this holiday by throwing water over each other on the street. People line up along the street and throw water over people walking by, but they also throw water at people in cars, on tuk-tuks and on bikes. It's like a national water fight. The only way to survive a drenching during Songkran is to stay at home. During Songkran 2002, just like every other year, hundreds of people lined up along Beach Road in Pattaya to throw water and enjoy the festivities. Everybody had buckets of water or huge water pistols to soak people passing by, and some people even hooked up hoses to the fire hydrants. These hoses shot out big jets of water. One day during Songkran, Tim was driving along Beach Road on his way to his bar, when he was knocked off his bike by one of these jets of water. Tim had been going quite slowly, so he only suffered a few scratches along his right leg and right arm, but Tim was furious. He snapped. He dragged the bike to the side of the road and stamped on it, once, twice, three times out of pure frustration. Then he threw his helmet on the ground and walked off, leaving his precious bike on its side at the side of the road.

Tim walked back to his bar. He still hadn't calmed down yet, so Gin asked him why he looked so angry. While shouting and waving his hands, he told Gin about the accident. When Gin heard that Tim had left the bike at the side of the road, she rushed off to retrieve it. While she was gone, Tim sat at the bar and poured himself a glass of Lao Khao whiskey, and then another and another. He hoped that the Lao Khao would help him calm down, but it didn't work. Thirty minutes later, Gin had still not come back. Tim walked towards Beach Road. When Gin came back to the bar with the bike, she gave Tim a call, but he didn't answer. He wasn't much of a phone person, so this wasn't unusual for him. Tim didn't come back to the bar that afternoon. At about 5:30 the police came to talk to Gin. They explained to her that Tim had gone to a hotel on Beach Road, got passed the reception, taken the lift up to the top and threw himself off the roof. He was gone.

I didn't find out until late that night, when someone told me a bar owner in Soi 8 had done this, and another customer came later and told me it was Tim. I went around to the bar but it was closed. Three days later, Gin opened the bar again. When I went to see her, she looked totally normal. 'He's gone now,' she said. 'Now I must make the business good.'

Tim's money stayed in America. Gin was not his wife, so she had no claim to it. After the day of Tim's death, his bike was never seen in Pattaya again. I don't know what Gin did with it. Gin carried on as if nothing happened and then she left Pattaya when the lease for the bar finished.

I got to know Tim reasonably well during his time in Pattaya. He was a lovely guy who had been through a lot of difficulties in his life. It was sad to see him turn to drink. You see this so many times in bars in Pattaya; people get caught up with the dream of living in Thailand, and owning a bar is one way to do it. But unless you have self-control and are very careful, drink, drugs or girls can take hold of you. Before you know it, your life starts spiralling out of control. Tim's suicide was the incident in particular that made me cut down on drinking and eventually leave the bar scene. During my two years in Pattaya, I knew several farangs who took their own life. Pattaya can eat people up. It's a fun city when things are going well, but it's a cruel, unforgiving place when things are not going your way.

The Price of Beauty

I first met Shane a few days before I was due to start working as a bar manager in Pattaya. I was having a quiet beer on my own on Second Road when he pulled up outside the bar on a Honda 500 Shadow. I had rented that very same bike for two weeks to explore Pattaya, and I had just returned it to the bike rental store earlier that day. Shane sat at the bar a few stools down from me. I complimented him on his choice of bike and we started chatting. We hit it off straight away. Shane was from Australia and he was in his mid-thirties. He was over six foot tall, he had an athletic build and he was a very good-looking guy. Shane didn't wear any jewellery or fancy clothes. He always wore a T-shirt, shorts and a pair of flip-flops like a lot of other farangs in Pattaya. But it soon became apparent that Shane was very wealthy. Years ago his father built a sixty-unit apartment block in Sydney and instead of selling them, he rented them all out. When his father passed away, Shane inherited the apartments, so I can only imagine how much money he was getting every month. He also used to own a large, successful bar in Sydney, but he had recently sold it and he was considering buying a bar in Pattaya. Shane was interested to hear that I would start managing a bar in a few days. We exchanged numbers and I told him to come for a drink in my bar when it opened.

Shane was one month into his six-month stay in Pattaya. He was staying in a five-star hotel along Beach Road, in a beautiful room right next to the hotel swimming pool. He paid for six months up front, so he must have got a good deal. I met up with Shane a couple of times before I started working as a bar manager. We usually went for a few beers and played pool together. I know that every farang who walks the streets of Pattaya gets a lot of attention from girls, but Shane got attention on a completely different scale to the rest of us. When we walked along the street, freelancers often tried to talk with Shane and link arms with him. Girls in bars and along the streets were constantly calling out 'handsome guy' and I knew they weren't talking about me. Whenever we walked into a beer bar, the girls were all over him. I was suddenly invisible. Shane was a Thai girl's dream guy – tall, handsome and rich.

One time I asked him, 'Do you often go with girls?'

'Hardly ever,' he said.

I found it a bit unusual that a guy getting all that attention from beautiful young women didn't give into temptation more often. I even wondered if he might be gay.

I started working in the bar and I didn't see Shane for about a week. Then one evening he turned up at my bar hand in hand with a beautiful Thai woman.

'Simon, this is Gee, my girlfriend,' he said, proudly.

I could understand the proud smirk on his face because Gee was stunningly beautiful. She had a curvy body, long jet-black hair, pouty lips and big bright eyes. Gee knew one of the girls working in the bar so they played pool together while Shane told me about how he met Gee.

Shane didn't go to go-go bars often, but a couple of days earlier he must have been bored. He was strolling down Soi 13, enjoying the party atmosphere, when he suddenly got the urge to go into a go-go bar and watch dozens of women dancing on a stage in bikinis. Shane sat down near the back and ordered a beer. He scanned the room and saw a farang couple talking to one of the working girls in the corner, and he saw an old farang near the stage looking up intently at the dancers. Only after looking at the other customers in the bar did Shane look at the dancers on the stage. There were five girls dancing; four of them looked very similar, Shane thought, and one of them stood out because she had short hair, but none of them interested Shane much. While he was drinking his beer, the five dancers stepped down and five new girls took their place on the stage. Shane was immediately drawn to one of the new dancers. She was taller than the other girls, and, in Shane's eyes, she was far more beautiful than the others. Shane immediately fell for her. He called over the mamasan and asked to talk with the beautiful tall dancer in the middle.

'Number 51?' The mamasan asked.

Shane looked closer and saw a pink badge with the number 51 attached to the lower part of her bikini.

'Yes, number 51.'

The mamasan signalled for number 51 to come and sit with Shane.

When she sat alongside Shane, he asked: 'What's your name? I don't want to call you 51.'

'My name is Gee,' she said, looking him up and down. 'You very handsome.'

The mamasan leant over and said to Shane, 'You buy her lady drink, okay?'

'Okay.'

The mamasan left Shane and Gee to talk alone. Gee was from a poor area up in northeast Thailand and she had only been working on the bar scene for six months, so her English was not very good. Despite the language barrier, Shane and Gee got along very well from the start – they clicked.

After only a few minutes, Shane called over the mamasan again and asked: 'How much to take Gee out of the bar?'

'Barfine is …'

'No, not barfine,' Shane interrupted, 'I mean, how much to take her out of the bar forever?'

The mamasan was shocked. 'No, no, no,' she said, shaking her head. 'No possible.'

Gee didn't understand what Shane had said, so the mamasan let her know in Thai. When Gee learnt what Shane had said, she laughed awkwardly and reached for her lady drink.

'Can you ask your manager?' Shane asked the mamasan.

The mamasan headed for the backroom, and as she passed the stage, she told the dancers what Shane had said. They all looked over at him in disbelief and one of them shouted out to Shane: 'Why you no take me?'

A few minutes later the owner of the go-go bar appeared. He was a stubborn-looking, middle-aged Thai guy with good English.

'What's the problem?' he asked Shane.

'I'm taking this girl out of the bar for good and I want to pay you,' Shane announced.

'No. You cannot do that,' the owner said. 'You have to pay her bar fine per day.'

Shane took out his wallet and counted out fifty thousand baht (over a thousand U.S. dollars).

'No, no,' the owner protested.

'I'm taking her out of the bar,' Shane insisted, as he handed the owner the money. 'You can take the money or leave it.'

Shane told Gee to get dressed and get her things. He finished his beer while he waited. The mamasan, the owner and all the girls in the bar were stunned by what had just happened. Gee emerged from the backroom fully dressed and carrying a small handbag. Shane stood up and led her out of the bar. The 50,000 baht must have included the price of the two drinks, because Shane didn't pay his bill.

I was astounded when Shane told me this story. I had never heard of anybody doing something like that before. But he was a bit silly really because he didn't need to pay the owner anything. Gee could have just quit her job on the spot. When Shane and Gee left the go-go bar, they went back to Shane's room and spent the night together. The next day Shane sent Gee to her pick up her stuff and move in with him. Shane never told me the sums involved, but he gave Gee money and explained that he wanted her to stay with him so that they could get to know each other better. Gee happily agreed – it beat working in a go-go bar for a living.

After Shane brought Gee to my bar, I started bumping into them a couple of times a week along Beach Road. I used to wake up early and go for a cheap English breakfast near the beach. Shane and Gee woke up early every morning to go for a swim in the sea. I was surprised to hear that Gee went for a swim every morning, because almost all of the Thai women I have ever met could not swim and hated going into the water, but Gee was keen to follow Shane's routine. After their swim, Shane and Gee used to get a massage from a couple of old women on the beach for about fifty baht each. They kept to that same routine every morning, and if they happened to bump into me after the massage, they joined me for breakfast. It was a struggle to involve Gee in the conversation sometimes because her English was poor. To help Gee learn English quickly and to help their relationship, Shane found a Thai woman with excellent English to tutor Gee five times a week. It couldn't have been cheap paying for a private tutor five times a week, but Shane knew that if Gee learned English quickly, it would help their relationship.

As well as sometimes meeting Shane and Gee in the morning, they often came to my bar in the evening to chat with me and the other girls, and to play pool. That bar was very dark and I used to get fed up being stuck in there all day, so whenever Shane visited me, we went outside for a couple of hours. He left Gee in the bar, which I thought was strange because guys in the bar might hit on her. But he trusted her completely. Shane and I used to walk around looking for potential bars for Shane to buy, and we often stopped somewhere for a beer and something to eat. I was new to the bar game, so Shane gave me a lot of helpful advice about how to attract customers and get them spending more. He was a great help to me in those early months.

Months passed and Shane couldn't find a bar that he liked. He was a very picky buyer because everything had to be perfect. He wanted a large bar in a great location, but all the bars available at the time were either too small or on a quiet soi. By Shane's last month in Thailand, Gee's English had improved a lot. Her pronunciation was much clearer than before and she was using full sentences with good grammar. Gee had also started to wear a lot of expensive designer clothes. Shane didn't like to wear expensive brands himself, but he wanted the best of everything for Gee. Shane bought her a couple of pairs of designer sunglasses too, but he noticed that she didn't wear them much. One day Gee told Shane that she was not happy with her nose.

'I want a big nose like foreigner so I can wear sunglasses,' she said.

Gee put on sunglasses to demonstrate the problem for Shane. He realized the problem straight away. The bridge of Gee's nose was too low, so the sunglasses fell off easily. Gee told Shane that she wanted an operation to make the bridge on her nose higher, 'same western women' she said. Gee thought it would make wearing sunglasses more comfortable, but more importantly she thought it would make her more beautiful. When Shane told me about this, I wasn't too surprised. Several of the girls working in the bar had told me that they wanted to have their noses done.

Shane agreed to pay for Gee's nose job, but instead of going to a hospital in Pattaya to get it done, he brought her to a famous hospital in Bangkok and paid top dollar. The girls in my bar told me a nose job only costs about one hundred and fifty dollars, but Shane paid almost a thousand dollars – only the best for Gee. Shane and Gee stayed in Bangkok for a week, and when they came back to Pattaya, Gee was wearing a bandage and there was some bruising around her nose. The bandage was removed a week later and they came to my bar to show off the results of the surgery.

To me, it didn't look right. Gee's new nose looked too high and slightly unnatural alongside her other facial features. If anything, Gee's new nose took away from her natural beauty. Of course I couldn't say any of this to Shane and Gee. I kept my mouth shut. They were both delighted with how her new nose looked and from that day on Gee wore sunglasses every day.

Shane's six months in Thailand came to an end. He had to go back to Australia for three months and then he would come back to Thailand for another six months. Shane knew he would be busy with his business in Australia, so he decided not to take Gee with him. Instead, he paid for the same hotel room for Gee for three months and he paid her English tutor in advance for three months too. Shane also gave Gee a generous allowance so that she could live comfortably while he was away.

I lived in a room directly above the bar, and some mornings I used to walk down to Beach Road and walk along the beach to clear my head. I often saw Gee having breakfast or coffee in one of the restaurants along the beach, just like she used to do with Shane. I sometimes had a coffee with Gee and I was amazed by how quickly her English was improving. She must have been studying a lot. She was able to tell stories and express herself more. Gee looked very happy at that time, but I also sensed that she was bored. She had too much time on her hands, and she had nothing to do except go swimming and study English. So, I told her pop into my bar sometime to play pool. About a month before Shane was due back in Pattaya, Gee started coming to my bar almost every evening. For the first few weeks she used to just have a beer or two, play pool with the girls in the bar and then go home early. But then there were a few times when Gee got very drunk, and another girl and I had to carry her back to her room. It was obvious that Gee was missing Shane. She was drinking out of loneliness and boredom. Shane came back to Pattaya just in time. I told him that Gee had been drunk a few times and that he shouldn't leave her alone next time. Shane agreed. He said he planned to bring Gee to Australia with him next time.

Shane and Gee started coming to my bar every day. Shane was a rich guy, but he wasn't flash with his money. He often bought drinks for his friends and some of the girls working in the bar, but he didn't ring the bell every night or anything like that. He was generous without being extravagant. When Shane and Gee came to my bar, they usually sat and chatted with me and the mamasan when they weren't playing pool. I will always remember one of the chats we had in particular. It was a quiet evening in the bar and we got on to the subject of Gee's breasts. Don't ask me how. Shane was thirty-five at the time and Gee was no more than twenty-seven. She had a great figure, so I was surprised when she said, 'Maybe I will get breast surgery.'

'Why?' the mamasan asked.

'My breasts are starting to sag.'

I had heard all sorts since I had started working in Pattaya as a bar manager, but this conversation even made me feel uncomfortable, perhaps because her boyfriend was sitting right next to me. I looked at Shane. Surprisingly, he seemed fine talking about his girlfriend's breasts with us.

'What you think, Shane?' the mamasan asked.

'Yes, I'm all for it,' he replied.

'I bet you are,' I said, and we both laughed. 'But how could her breasts be sagging already? She's too young.'

Gee lifted up her T-shirt suddenly and showed us her breasts. I didn't know where to look, but seeing that Shane and the mamasan were staring intently at Gee's breasts, I decided to have a good look too. Her breasts were beautiful, large, brown and plump. Shane was a lucky man. After we all had a good look, I thought Gee would pull her T-shirt down again, but instead she asked me and the mamasan to touch her breasts. She wanted us to feel the weight and the shape, and then give our opinion about whether she needed surgery or not. The mamasan and I had a feel of one breast each; I took the left one, the mamasan took the right one.

'I don't think you need surgery,' I said to Gee.

I'm not sure which way the mamasan voted, but she called over one of the girls in the bar, Nui, who had already had breast surgery. Nui came over and without hesitation she lifted up her top and asked us all to feel her breasts. I stopped participating at this point, but Shane, the mamasan and Gee spent the next few minutes feeling both sets of breasts and comparing them in great detail. The conclusion they finally came to was that Gee needed surgery to firm up her breasts, but not to make them bigger.

According to Nui, breast surgery cost five or six hundred in any of the big hospitals in Pattaya, but Shane brought Gee back to the expensive hospital in Bangkok and he paid three thousand dollars. A few weeks after the surgery, they both walked into my bar and Gee proudly whipped up her T-shirt to show us her new and improved breasts. She was delighted with the results.

'Simon, feel,' Gee instructed me.

To be fair, her breasts felt much firmer now, and they were clearly bigger.

Gee went over to Nui and the other girls to show off her breasts. I turned to Shane and said: 'They are bigger. I thought she was only going to get them firmed up.'

'Yes, but we thought while she is getting them firmed up, why not get them enlarged a bit too,' Shane answered, with a big grin on his face.

He looked like a very happy man.

Shane decided against getting a bar in Pattaya. After considering the price of a bar in a good location and the money he could expect to make from it every month, he figured it wasn't worth his time or effort. Now that he was no longer looking for a bar in Pattaya, Shane decided to travel around Thailand with Gee. They flew down to Krabi and spent a week there. Then they came back to Pattaya for a week and then flew up to Chiang Mai. They travelled like this for about three months, using Pattaya as their base. They had a great life and they looked really happy together. During Shane's last month in Thailand, he arranged a tourist visa for Gee. This time he brought Gee with him to Australia.

They reappeared in Pattaya three months later – same hotel, same room. On their first day back, Shane told me: 'While we were in Australia, Gee told me she doesn't think she is beautiful.'

'But she is beautiful,' I said. It was obvious.

'I think she is beautiful too, but she doesn't. She has no confidence. She wants to get more surgery done.'

I almost rolled my eyes in front of Shane, but I managed to control myself.

'What does she want to get done now?' I asked.

'Botox,' he said. 'It's not even surgery, it's a procedure. But she also thinks that her chin is too sharp so she is thinking about getting her chin shaved.'

'Mate, she doesn't need any more surgery,' I told him. 'She is a beautiful girl. When will it be enough?'

'I know,' he said, deep in thought, 'but she thinks it will make her feel beautiful. And if she feels good about herself, it will give her confidence and make her happier.'

Off they went to Bangkok again. They stayed in Bangkok for five or six weeks while Gee got the course of Botox injections. When they came back to my bar, I was surprised by the results. Gee had gotten Botox at the top of her cheeks, and, to be honest, it made her look a bit strange. This time neither Gee nor Shane mentioned anything about the Botox, so perhaps they weren't completely happy with how it looked either. The following month, they went back to Bangkok and Gee got her chin bone shaved down. Apparently her chin was too pointy and she wanted it flattened. They came back to Pattaya a month later and when they walked into my bar I thought, oh my god, you are starting to look like a man. Her beauty was gone. She had a flat chin, two ping pong balls in her upper cheek and a witch's nose. But of course I couldn't say anything to Gee or Shane.

About a month before they were due to go back to Australia, Gee decided that she needed more Botox in her cheeks to match her new chin. It was time for another trip to Bangkok. I didn't expect to see either of them for the next month, but a few days later Shane walked into my bar looking distressed.

'What's wrong?' I asked him. 'Why are you back so soon?'

'Something went wrong with the Botox,' he said. 'I just came back to get some more of Gee's stuff.'

'What went wrong?'

'Gee's left cheek got infected. The doctors said they will have to take part of her cheek away to get rid of the infection.'

I could see that Shane was distraught, and I could only imagine what Gee was going through. I felt so sorry for them both.

'What will happen after they take away part of her cheek?' I asked.

'They might be able to reconstruct it or put in more Botox, but it might never look the same again.'

I could see that Shane was terribly worried about Gee. I put my hand on his shoulder to show my support, and we sat in silence for a few minutes because neither of us had anything more to add. It was a sad situation and all we could do now was hope that Gee got better soon.

About four months later Shane and Gee came back to Pattaya. When I saw Gee, I felt so sad for her. The surgery had gone all wrong. Her face was a mess. One cheek was enlarged by the Botox and the other cheek was concave, and of course she still had the weird nose and flat chin. I controlled my reactions as I went over and greeted both Gee and Shane warmly. Apart from her appearance, I noticed other changes in Gee too. She was not bubbly and outgoing like she used to be. She was now subdued and quiet. Also, when Gee used to come to my bar before, she would always talk and joke a lot with the other girls in the bar, but this time she always stuck very close to Shane. It kind of looked like she was hiding behind him.

Over the next six months, the doctors did their best to

reconstruct Gee's cheek. Gee also got an eyelift during that time. An eyelift! She was still in her twenties! When I saw Gee after the latest rounds of surgery, I was shocked. The eyelift was a disaster, so now one eyebrow looked higher than the other. It looked weird. But worst of all, the reconstruction surgery had not gone well. The left cheek was no longer concave, but it was an odd shape and much smaller than her right cheek. Needless to say, Shane and Gee were not happy with the results, but the doctors refused to carry out any more procedures on Gee. She had turned into a Frankenstein figure – a victim of plastic surgery gone wrong. She looked deformed – one eyebrow higher than the other, one cheek bigger and rounder than the other, an oddly flat chin and an oddly high nose.

Shane and Gee decided to leave Thailand and go live in Australia. Around that time I quit my job in the bar and moved to Bangkok. Shane and I kept in contact by email. About a year after they moved to Australia, they got married and Shane sent me some wedding photos. From the photos, I could clearly see that Gee had gotten more surgery on her face, but if anything it made her look even worse. Over the years I gradually lost contact with Shane, but I heard from a friend of a friend that Shane and Gee are still happily married in Australia.

It was sad to see Gee become a victim of plastic surgery like that, and it was amazing to think that such a naturally beautiful girl could struggle with confidence. As for Shane, I always thought it was great how he stuck by Gee and supported her through it all. A lesser guy might have walked away. Are there any lessons to be learned from Gee's misfortune? Sure. If your girlfriend asks for a nose job so she can wear sunglasses, just say no.

Love On Beach Road

A lot of people have the preconception that most of the farangs who visit Pattaya are old, retired and looking for love. Well, Mike was old and retired, but he wasn't exactly looking for love. He got divorced in his late fifties, and when he was in his early sixties he came to Thailand for the first time. He came back to Pattaya two more times over the next couple of years. On his third trip to Pattaya he ended up strolling into my bar one quiet evening. He sat at the bar and kept himself to himself. A few of the girls tried to strike up a conversation with him, but he politely explained that he would like to be alone. He was the only customer in the bar, so when I saw him order a second beer, I asked him if he'd like to have a game of pool with me. His face lit up. Like myself, Mike loved a game of pool. We hit it off right away and we've stayed in touch ever since.

Mike loved Pattaya so much that he decided it would be the perfect place to retire. At the age of sixty-five, he put most of his belongings into storage and moved to Thailand. I helped him find a nice condo and he already had a few friends in Pattaya, so he settled into his new life very easily.

Mike found himself sitting on a bench along Beach Road in Pattaya one evening. His friend had left him to go drink beer and shoot pool with bargirls. Mike wasn't really into that side of Pattaya; he was happier just to sit on his own and appreciate the beautiful sunset play out in front of him. Pattaya is famous for its sex tourism, but that wasn't why Mike chose to retire there. He chose Pattaya because it's by the ocean, there are a lot of farangs and countless restaurants with good western food. Just because he was living in Pattaya didn't mean that he had to go to a beer bar every night and barfine a girl. He had been in Pattaya for two months already and he had been with a handful of girls already, but that was enough for him. He didn't want to be one of those farangs who got blind drunk every night in those girlie bars, nor did he want to be one of those hapless guys who fell for a bargirl and lost everything. He was too old for all that. At sixty-five years old, all he wanted was for his retired life to be calm and relaxing. But this is Pattaya.

Mike watched the people pass by. He saw a lot of beautiful young Thai women with much older western guys. He saw single men walking along the beach aimlessly, and he saw a lot of freelancers (both women and ladyboys) prowling for customers. One woman stuck out among all these people, because she was very tall for a Thai woman and she was wearing an elegant, slim-fitting white dress. Her long silky black hair reached down almost to her waist. She was leaning against a tree about ten meters to

Mike's left. This woman was looking out at the ocean while she slowly drank a bottle of mineral water through a straw. That struck Mike as unusual. He observed her for several minutes, and finally she looked his way and met his eyes. She smiled warmly at Mike before turning back to the ocean and placing the straw between her lips again. Mike was very attracted to this woman, but she was very tall so he thought she might be a ladyboy. Curiosity got the best of him and he decided to go over and introduce himself.

'Hello, I'm Mike,' he said. 'What's your name?'

'My name is Kung,' she replied, in a very feminine voice. 'Nice to meet you.'

Mike was five foot ten, and now that he was standing alongside Kung, he could see that she was only a few inches shorter than him.

'You are very tall,' he blurted out.

'Yes, some people think I am a ladyboy because I am so tall,' Kung said, and laughed. 'But I'm not.'

Mike was hoping to chat with Kung for a while, but she suddenly said she had to leave.

'I hope to see you again,' she said, as she walked off, and before she crossed the road she turned back and smiled at Mike.

Mike walked back to his rented condo, and for the rest of the evening all he could think about was Kung. He had never seen a Thai woman wear that kind of dress; she looked so sophisticated. He recalled over and over again how her body swayed from side to side when she walked away from him. The moment she turned back to him and smiled was vivid in his mind. And her English! She was fluent. But why did she leave so suddenly? He asked himself. Most other women along Beach Road would have asked him for money to take them to a short-time room. So this girl isn't a bargirl or a freelancer? This question kept him awake into the early hours of the morning.

The following evening Mike cancelled his plan to meet his friend so that he could go back to the beach and look for Kung. He arrived there at 4 pm and sat in the same spot as the previous day. He waited for two hours without any luck, but at about 6 pm he was delighted to see Kung walk towards him. Mike stood up and greeted Kung. He asked her to sit with him on the bench. Mike was overexcited so he started bombarding Kung with questions. She was open at the start, and she told Mike that she was forty-two years old, but she was not married and she didn't have any children.

'And what do you do for a living?' he asked, paying particular attention to this answer.

'I am not working now,' she said, 'but I used to work in the massage industry for twenty years.'

Massage industry? It is such a vague term in Thailand. It can mean anything. She could have been a soapy massage girl who massaged her customers in a bath and then slept with them, or she could have been a genuine masseuse. Mike didn't know what to think.

Kung soon started steering the conversation away from her and towards Mike. It didn't take much prodding to get Mike to spew out his whole life story. Within minutes she knew that Mike was American and divorced, that he didn't have children, that he used to work in the financial market and that he was in Thailand to live long-term. The only topic Mike purposefully avoided was money. He knew better than to tell her that his pension was two thousand dollars a month, and that he had 320,000 U.S. dollars (about ten million baht) in savings. But he was an open book about everything else.

Similar to the previous day, Kung suddenly said that she had to go somewhere, but before she walked off, Mike asked her if he could bring her for dinner the following evening.

'Not in the evening. I have plans,' she said. 'But I can meet tomorrow at about one o'clock for lunch.'

Mike was delighted. They exchanged phone numbers and agreed to meet at the same spot the next day at one o' clock.

Mike and Nung met the next day on Beach Road, and Nung led him to a nearby restaurant that she liked. Ever the gentleman, Mike pulled out the chair for Kung to sit down. He sat down across from her and stared at her for a minute while she looked through the menu. She was dressed in a beautiful red dress this time and her long black hair was tied back. Dressed in shorts and a T-shirt, Mike regretted not wearing a shirt. They both ordered pasta for lunch, and while they were waiting for their food, Mike thought it would be a good time to get to know more about Kung. She knew almost everything about him, but she was still a mystery. Instead of bombarding her with questions like the previous day, he casually said: 'Kung, tell me a little bit about your life. How did you end up in Pattaya?'

Kung instantly looked uncomfortable with this question.

'I'm sorry, but I don't like to share personal information with people I don't really know.'

That put a stop to Mike's plan. Mike was in unknown territory. He had never met a Thai woman like this. The only Thai women he had spoken to at length were bargirls and freelancers, and those types of women were brash and they never refused to answer anything. They were always ready to paint a quick picture of their life for their farang customer, but Mike was now faced with a reserved Thai woman who was worried about opening up too much. This made her all the more beautiful to Mike. Throughout the meal they talked about their favourite spots in Pattaya. Kung had lived there for twenty years, so she knew the area well. She told Mike about some nice lakes and parks outside of the city that were worth visiting.

The meal was nice and Mike enjoyed Kung's company. While they were waiting for the bill, Mike couldn't contain his emotions or his lust anymore.

'Kung, I think you are amazing and I want to be with you,' he said, placing his hand on hers across the table. 'If I give you 2000 baht, will you come back to my condo?'

Two thousand was twice as much as a bargirl would expect to get from a customer. In Mike's head it was a good offer.

Kung sighed deeply and shook her head, like she had just wasted an hour of her life.

'You have misunderstood me completely, Mike,' she said, and then she grabbed her bag and stood up to leave.

Mike jumped out of his chair.

'Wait! Please, wait,' he pleaded. 'I'm sorry. I didn't mean to offend you.'

'I'm not that kind of girl,' she said, with a stern look on her face. 'If you want that kind of girl, they are easy to find in Pattaya, but I never go with farang for money.'

'Okay. Okay. I'm sorry. Please sit down.'

Mike was terrified that Kung would walk out the door and never talk to him again. He didn't want to blow his chance with this woman.

'Please, sit down.'

Kung sighed again and her face softened. She sat back down.

'It's okay,' she said. 'I understand. A lot of farang come to Pattaya and think they can buy any girl. Maybe I gave you the wrong idea.'

Mike was relieved that she didn't leave, and he started

blabbering on about his feelings towards her and about how different she was to the other women in Pattaya. Kung listened to Mike, but she didn't say anything about her feelings towards him.

When Mike and Kung left the restaurant, they went for a walk along Beach Road.

'Do you have family?' Mike asked, as they walked along leisurely with the beach and the ocean to their left.

'My parents died when I was quite young, but I have one brother. He is working in a clothes store on the other side of Pattaya.'

'I see. And do you work?'

'No, I'm not working,' Kung replied. 'I've got a bit of money and I'm looking to set up my own business and then my brother can come work for me.'

Mike was intrigued. 'What kind of business?'

'I'd really like to get a guesthouse – somewhere nice where I can settle down with someone.'

'Settle down?'

'Yes, I'd really like to find a partner as I get older.' Kung answered, now starting to open up a little.

After walking for quarter of an hour in the afternoon sun, Kung said that she had to go somewhere. She agreed to meet Mike the next day at 3 pm for a coffee. Mike leant forward to give Kung a kiss goodbye on the cheek, but she pulled away sheepishly and held out her hand for a handshake instead.

That evening Mike came to my bar for a few beers. He told me all about Kung, and he even said that he was starting to fall in love with her.

'Come on. Get a grip, mate,' I said. 'You met this girl on Beach Road in the evening wearing a dress. What are you doing?'

'I don't think she is a bargirl or a freelancer,' Mike responded.

'But you know the kind of girls that hang around Beach Road.'

'I know, but this woman is different.'

I shook my head in disbelief. I had never seen this side of Mike before. He was usually very cautious and a little cynical when it came to the local women, yet here he was falling for a girl he met on Beach Road.

Mike and Kung met each other for a few hours in the afternoon for the next three days, and then on the fourth day Kung suddenly suggested going to Bangkok because she wanted to do some shopping. Bangkok was only a couple of hours away in a taxi, so Mike went along with it. They ended up booking into a hotel in Bangkok and they spent the night together for the first time. Mike couldn't believe his luck. He had managed to hook up with this beautiful, special woman. He had never known feelings or passion like this. After their night together in Bangkok, Mike thought they would become an official couple, but in the taxi on their way back to Pattaya, Mike asked Kung what she would like to eat for dinner, and she surprised him with her answer:

'I can't have dinner with you this evening,' she said, a little awkwardly. 'To be honest, I don't think we should see each other for a few days. I need some time to think about things. I'll call you in a few days and we can have lunch.'

Mike was disappointed, but he knew that he had to give her space. Kung didn't want the taxi to drop her off at her home. Instead, she asked the driver to drop her off on Beach Road and then bring Mike to his condo.

A few days later, Kung called Mike and asked him to meet her for lunch in a seafood restaurant on Walking Street. On his way to the restaurant, Mike felt very nervous. He knew that this could go one of two ways: either Kung would put an end to their relationship before it started or she would suggest starting their relationship in earnest. Kung was already there when Mike arrived. She was sitting at a table out in the decking area overlooking the water. Right after they ordered food, Mike came straight out with it and asked: 'Did you think a lot about us?'

'Yes,' Kung replied, very composed. 'I'm getting feelings towards you that I've never had before. It's a little strange and I'm a little scared. I don't want to hurt you and I don't want to get hurt.'

'I won't hurt you,' Mike interrupted.

'What do you think we should do?' Kung asked Mike. 'Do you think we should stop now or go forward together?'

'I want to be with you,' Mike said passionately. 'I've wanted to be with you since the first day I saw you leaning against the tree on Beach Road.'

'But you know I want to get a guesthouse. I think it would work well if we ran it together. Next week I will go to Koh Samui. I've never been there before, but I heard it is a beautiful island. It has an international airport and it's a popular place for tourists, so that's where I would like to get a guesthouse. Would you like to come with me?'

'To Koh Samui?'

Mike was not expecting this.

'Yes.'

'For how long?'

'I'm not sure. Maybe two or three weeks. I want to get to know the area and maybe look for some properties that are available.'

Mike took a moment to think about how he should word his response.

'Kung, I came to Thailand to retire. I never thought about getting a business here, but then again I never thought about falling for a woman either, but I have. Look, this is a lot for me to take in. I'm not sure how I feel about the business idea yet. All I know is that I want to be with you. So how about this: we go to Koh Samui together and we enjoy our holiday. We can take things slow and see how we feel about the business later.'

Kung agreed with Mike's plan.

The next week Mike and Kung flew down to Koh Samui. They booked into a beautiful four-star hotel by Chaweng Beach – the busiest area in Koh Samui. As soon as they checked into the hotel and got to their room, they had daytime sex. It was only their second time sleeping together. After that, they showered and Kung suggested going for a walk along the beach before it got dark. She threw on a pair of shorts, a T-shirt, a pair of sunglasses and a sun hat. This was the first time Mike saw her wear anything other than a dress, and she looked stunning. Mike was in love – no doubt about it. He had no chance of getting out of this now. He felt so lucky to have found this amazing woman. And to think that he found her on Beach Road, Pattaya! What a stroke of luck.

Mike and Kung spent their first week in Koh Samui enjoying the beach, going for nice meals, and relaxing by the pool. It was like a honeymoon. Neither of them had been to Koh Samui before, but they both agreed that it was paradise. The beach was cleaner than in Pattaya, and sex tourism, although still present, was not as prevalent. Mike and Kung enjoyed their first week in Samui so much that they didn't even go out looking for available properties. Then one evening over dinner, Kung opened up to Mike and said 'I am having an amazing time. I have completely fallen for you. I don't want this to end.'

'Me too,' Mike said. 'This is the happiest I have ever been in my life. Let's stay in this hotel for another few weeks. We can hire scooters and go explore the island, and we can look for properties for the guesthouse.'

Kung was delighted to hear Mike mention the guesthouse on his own.

The next day they hired two scooters. They were four hundred baht each per day. Kung paid and she gave her ID card for it to be scanned in case anything happened to the scooters. On their third day of exploring the island, Mike and Kung were coming back to Chaweng Beach by a different road and a building with a 'For Sale' sign caught Kung's eye. It was a three-storey building with a reception area and three stores on the ground floor. All the stores were open for business but the reception area was closed.

'That would make a nice guesthouse,' Kung said.

'It looks a bit run down,' Mike observed.

'But we could make it nice again,' Kung insisted, as she saved the number of the realtor in her phone.

When they got back to the hotel, Kung rang the realtor and arranged a viewing of the building for the following morning.

When the realtor showed Mike and Kung around the property, he said in broken English: 'It guesthouse before. Five rooms for guests, and in back small condo for owners to live. The old owners like large reception area, but you can make bar there too, no problem.'

'What's the asking price?' Mike asked.

'The owners want six million baht,' the realtor replied. 'Samui is expensive. It is very popular island.'

After the realtor left, Mike and Kung walked around the area to get a sense of the property's location. The location was very good. It was situated about two hundred meters from the beach and there were a lot of restaurants and bars in between. It was a lively area, and it was only half a kilometre from the main nightlife area in Chaweng Beach.

Mike and Kung sat in an air-conditioned café and ordered a coffee.

'You love it, don't you?' Mike said to Kung, seeing that she could barely contain her excitement.

'Yes, I love it,' Kung said. 'It's exactly the kind of place I was looking for. Five rooms upstairs, a nice condo for us to live in. We can make a bar downstairs and do some other business at the front of the guesthouse. But it's expensive so I need to look at the money and think about the finances.'

'How much do you think the building is really worth?' Mike asked.

He still didn't know how much money Kung had. He kept asking himself, does she expect me to put money into this?

Kung took a few minutes to work out some numbers on a piece of paper, and then she told Mike,

'If we could get it for four million and then spend another million doing it up, then we could get it up and running as a guesthouse and slowly expand it.'

For the first time, Kung opened up about her financial

situation. She said, 'I have two million baht spare for a business, and I could go to the bank to get the rest of the money. But I have to consider you in all this too, Mike. Do you want to invest money and own this guesthouse with me, or do you just want to be my boyfriend?'

Mike asked Kung to run him through the numbers. He noticed straight away that she had a good business head and she was very good at explaining everything. Mike's background was in finance, so he knew what he was looking for, and he could see that this was a viable business. The only problem was that Mike was reluctant to come out of retirement. He expressed this concern to Kung.

'We can hire staff,' she said. 'We won't need to work a lot, especially not you. You can stay retired.'

Finally, Mike agreed to match Kung's two million baht, and then put in a further one million baht as a loan to the business, which meant they had five million baht to buy the building and do it up. Mike's logic was that in the worst-case scenario he would lose three million baht, and he was fine with that. A three million baht hit wouldn't break the bank.

Mike and Kung were a bit cheeky with their first bid on the property; they offered 3.5 million baht, but it was quickly rejected. Their second offer of four million baht was eventually accepted. Mike had to go back to his condo in Pattaya to get his bank stuff together and transfer the three million baht from his American bank account to his Thai bank account. After that, Kung brought Mike to a small law firm in Bangkok that she had used a few times in the past. The lawyer spoke excellent English and he explained to Mike and Kung all the paperwork that they would need to do. He explained that because Mike and Kung were not married, the guesthouse would have to be in Kung's name, but Mike could get a yellow book called a Tabien Baan to show that he was registered to the address of the guesthouse. By the recommendation of this lawyer, Mike and Kung also signed a document so that if they ever broke up, one would have to buy the other out, and they set the value of the business at five million baht. So, if anything went wrong, Mike would be able to get his three million baht back, or he could buy Kung out for two million baht. After a few days, the sale went through, all the paperwork was signed, and Mike and Kung were the proud owners of a guesthouse on Koh Samui. They took a couple of weeks to wrap up their lives in Pattaya and then moved down to Koh Samui to start a brand new life together. For me, it was sad to see Mike move away from Pattaya, and it was also a little worrying to see him go into business with a woman he hardly knew.

Mike and Kung hired a condo short term while the builders were in, renovating the guesthouse. There was a lot to arrange before the guesthouse was ready to open. They had to find an interior designer, a website designer, they had to stock the bar and find staff for both the bar and the hotel. Fortunately for

Mike, Kung took care of everything. Mike offered to help, but he couldn't speak Thai so he wasn't much use. A few weeks before the guesthouse was ready to open, Kung reminded Mike that she wanted her brother to come and work in the guesthouse. Mike had never met Kung's brother before, but he was fine with the idea. Kung's brother arrived a few days later and rented a cheap apartment about a kilometre from the guesthouse. He was a couple of years older than Kung, and he didn't speak English, but he seemed like a nice guy. He was hired as a receptionist and general handyman around the guesthouse.

Five weeks from when the renovation work started, the guesthouse was ready to open for business. It had only cost eight hundred thousand baht (two hundred thousand less than Mike and Kung had expected) to do up the guesthouse. They didn't hold an opening party; they simply opened the doors one morning and relied on walk-ins. The guesthouse looked new and clean so it started to attract customers from the start. The bar was very quiet during the day, but it did well in the evenings through to closing time. Both the guesthouse and the bar started making a healthy profit from the second month. A few weeks before high season started, Kung told Mike that they should use the space at the front of the guesthouse for renting out scooters.

'Let's get six scooters and rent them out,' she suggested. 'We are in a prime location. We can make money.'

They spent 600,000 baht on six scooters. They used the

200,000 baht left over from the renovation work, plus 400,000 baht from Mike's own money to pay for the scooters. They parked the six scooters outside the guesthouse next to a simple 'Bikes for rent' sign, and they soon started making money. Mike and Kung were delighted. It was such a simple, profitable business to set up. It all happened so quickly that Mike barely took a moment to consider that he was now set to lose 3.4 million baht if the worst came to the worst.

The first year of business went very smoothly for Mike and Kung. Their business was profitable and they were still very much in love. They had good staff, so, like Kung had promised, they didn't need to work long hours. They had plenty of time to go for romantic walks along the beach and go for a nice meal and a drink in the evenings. Everything was good in paradise.

One day Mike decided that he wanted to go back to Pattaya to catch up with me and some of his other friends; he had not been back there since he moved to Koh Samui. Kung thought it was a great idea for Mike to go meet his friends for a few days. Mike came to my bar three nights in a row. Especially when he had a few drinks in him, he explained how much he loved Kung and about how well the business was going. By that time I had already witnessed so many disastrous relationships between Thai women and farang men in Pattaya, so I was surprised to hear that Mike had been so lucky in love.

'I can't believe you met her on Beach Road,' I often remarked.

A few days later Mike returned to Koh Samui in the afternoon. He got a taxi to the guesthouse and went straight to the condo. Kung wasn't there. The woman at the reception said that she had gone to visit her brother. Mike jumped on a scooter and headed to the brother's apartment. It was one of half a dozen small, rundown apartments that lined a narrow backstreet. Mike pulled up in front of Kung's brother's house. The front door was slightly ajar. When Mike knocked, the door swung open. There was a small lounge area with a sofa and a TV, but it was empty. At the back of the lounge area there was a door that led to the bedroom and toilet. Mike walked through the lounge and found that this door was also slightly opened. This time he pushed the door open slowly. What did he see? He saw his worst nightmare right in front of his eyes. He saw Kung in bed with her 'brother'. Everything froze for a second when Mike and Kung made eye contact with each other. A few moments of stillness and silence was needed for everything to sink in. Kung suddenly gasped loudly and grabbed the duvet to cover her naked body. Then she went into defensive mode.

'What are you doing here?' she screamed at Mike. 'Why you walk into somebody else's home? You crazy?'

Still in utter shock, Mike turned around and walked out. At the front of the apartment he sat on the scooter and put his head in his hands in despair. He couldn't believe what he had just seen.

He couldn't move. Mike sat on the scooter for a minute, perhaps hoping that Kung would come out and say something to make him understand, but then he thought to himself, I've gotta get out of here. I can't be around these people anymore.

Mike drove back to the guesthouse and packed all his stuff. He got a taxi to the airport and booked a flight to Bangkok. Now that he had a ticket out of Koh Samui, he sat on a chair and took some time to reflect on what he had seen. He leant forward with his elbows resting on his knees and his face buried deep in his sweaty hands. He kept shaking his head in disbelief.

It was her boyfriend all along, he thought to himself, and then he tried to remember if he had seen anything unusual between Kung and this man before, but nothing came to mind. They had hidden it from him well. They must have been carrying on right under Mike's nose for the whole year.

'Mike.' A soft, sad voice interrupted his thoughts.

Mike lowered his hands and saw Kung standing in front of him. She sat down next to Mike. They didn't look at each other; they looked straight ahead at all the people passing by.

'I'm sorry, Mike,' she said. 'I'm very sorry. Where are you going?'

'I'm going to Bangkok,' Mike replied.

Calm and collected, Kung said to Mike: 'While you are in Bangkok, go the lawyers. I will pay you back all your money. I'm sorry.'

Kung stood up and walked away.

It was a short but difficult flight to Bangkok for Mike. The beautiful life he had been enjoying in Koh Samui had suddenly vanished, gone up in smoke. He wondered if the perfect life he was enjoying with Kung ever really existed. Wasn't it all just an illusion created by Kung? he thought. Now he was alone again without a home. He had friends in Pattaya but he was in no rush to go back there. He wasn't ready to tell his friends about how Kung's 'brother' turned out to be her lover. 'I'm not surprised, mate. You met her on Beach Road. What did you expect?', 'They are all the same', 'Farang are just walking ATM machines', 'They always have a Thai boyfriend hidden away somewhere.' Mike was worried he would hear these kinds of comments when he told his friends in Pattaya about Kung, because that's how most farangs in Pattaya talked about the local girls. Mike wasn't ready to listen to people tell him how foolish he had been, so he decided to stay away from Pattaya for a while. When he arrived in Bangkok he checked into a hotel in Sukhumvit and locked himself away in his room for the night.

The next day the lawyer assured Mike that all the paperwork was in order and that he had nothing to worry about.

'Are you sure you don't want to buy her out?' the lawyer asked.

'No,' Mike replied. 'Kung already said she will buy me out.'

'I will contact Kung, but it will take her at least a few days to get the money together. Will you be able to stay in Bangkok until we sort all this out?'

'Yes, I will be staying in Bangkok.'

A few days later, the lawyer asked Mike to drop by the office to have a look at the paperwork. But when Mike arrived at the lawyer's building, he was surprised to see Kung standing in the entrance waiting for him. Mike was shocked. He thought he would never see her again.

Mike and Kung went to a café nearby to talk. After they ordered coffee and took a seat, Kung took out two large piles of cash from her handbag. The pile of money in her right hand was much larger than the one in her left. She placed the two piles of money on the table and then looked up at Mike.

'I am very sorry, Mike,' Kung said, looking and sounding very heavy hearted. 'You must hate me.'

Mike didn't want any apologies. He wanted closure.

'Who is he?' he asked 'He's your boyfriend, isn't he? And you've been seeing him behind my back the whole time.'

'Mike, I know that you are a good man and I can trust you,' Kung said, removing her hands from the two piles of money and placing them on her lap. 'I have something to tell you, but you might not believe me.'

Kung paused for a moment to take a drink from her iced coffee. Only when she placed the straw between her lips, did Mike realize that Kung was wearing the same beautiful white dress that she was wearing when he first saw her on Beach Road.

'What I'm about to tell you, you can never tell anyone,' Kung said, very seriously. 'I've lived with this for a long time.'

Kung stopped and looked around to make sure that nobody was listening. There wasn't anyone within earshot, so she continued:

'The man you caught me with is not my brother. That man has been blackmailing me for many years for something I did a long time ago, something that was very bad.'

Mike immediately thought, what could she have done that was so bad?

'My real brother was a very bad man. He was very bad to me so I paid somebody to do something to his car, and then my brother crashed the car and died.'

Kung kept her head hung low as she told this to Mike. She was clearly ashamed of herself.

'The man you saw me with is the man I paid to do something to my brother's car. He has been blackmailing me ever since. He makes me have sex with him and give him money, and he always sticks close to me so that he can control me.'

Mike was stunned by Kung's story. He thought it was rubbish at first, but then he started to reconsider. Mike looked at Kung closely. He looked into her tear-filled eyes, and he saw her hold her left arm with her right arm to comfort herself. She was in pain. She looked vulnerable. Mike remembered how lovely Kung had always been to him. She never tried to squeeze money out of him or manipulate him in anyway. Her story was incredible, but nobody could make something like that up, he thought. It's such a crazy story that it might just be true.

When Mike started to consider that Kung might be the victim of this man's blackmail, he started to feel sympathy towards her. He started to look at Kung with loving eyes again.

'But how could you do that to your brother?' Mike asked Kung, suddenly remembering that she was not an innocent victim in all this.

'It was a mistake,' she said, shaking her head. 'My brother was a terrible man and he made my life like a nightmare. I was so angry with him that I wasn't thinking straight.'

This story made sense. Kung was special. She wouldn't go with other men. She must have been blackmailed. Mike's image of his lovely Kung was being restored.

'Mike, I love you, you know I do, and I want to spend my life with you,' Kung said intensely. 'I can fix this. I have three million baht here. The man said that if I give him one million baht, he will leave me alone and never come back again. He has never said anything like that before. I believe him. I will give two million baht to you, one million to him, and then I will sell the hotel and give you back the other one million that I owe you.'

Mike sat back and tried to take all this in.

'Let's sell the hotel in Samui and use the money to go

somewhere new,' Kung said, her voice suddenly full of hope and energy, 'somewhere nobody knows us. What do you think?'

'I don't know what to think,' Mike said, bemused. 'I really don't know what to think about all this. It's crazy.'

'I know,' Kung agreed. 'It's crazy. But please don't let it ruin our life together.'

Mike was starting to believe Kung, but he wasn't fully convinced yet. After they talked in the coffee shop, Mike and Kung went to the lawyers together. Kung gave Mike two million baht in cash and they instructed the lawyer to prepare paperwork to show that Kung now only owed Mike one million baht. Nobody mentioned the 400,000 baht that Mike had invested to buy the scooters for the guesthouse.

Kung ended up staying in Mike's hotel room that night, and Mike was introduced to the joys of make-up sex. When he woke up the next morning he reflected on everything that had happened with Kung. He decided that Kung deserved his trust; she had been forced into having sex with that man for all those years.

In the afternoon they went to the lawyers to sign the new paperwork. They spent a few romantic, passionate days and nights together in Bangkok, and then Kung went back to Koh Samui to pay off the man and sell the guesthouse. Instead of going with Kung to Samui, Mike decided to go to Pattaya. He needed to talk to a friend about the chaos he had just come through, so he turned up at my bar out of the blue. He told me all about Kung and the man who was blackmailing her. As you can imagine, I was shocked by it all, especially when I heard that Mike had slept with Kung again after everything that had happened.

'You cannot be involved with someone who has done this,' I said strongly. 'You got off lightly. Just walk away!'

'I know I should,' Mike said, 'but I still love her.'

Mike stayed in Pattaya for a few days, and during that time he decided that his next stop would be Phuket – a large island in the southeast of Thailand with a big tourist scene. He had never been to Phuket before, but he had heard a lot of good things about it. Mike flew down to Phuket and stayed in Patong, which is the biggest tourist spot on the island. On his third day in Phuket, Mike got a call from Kung. She said she found a Swedish guy who was interested in buying the guesthouse. Kung was asking for 7.5 million baht, but the Swedish guy was only offering 6.5 million. Mike and Kung had bought the guesthouse for 4 million and then spent a further 1.4 million on renovations and scooters, so the Swedish guy's 6.5 million baht offer meant a 1.1 million baht profit. Mike told Kung to accept the offer.

'I agree,' Kung said. 'But it will take a few weeks for the Swedish man to get all the money together, so I will stay in Samui until then. When the sale goes through, I will go to you in Phuket.'

'What happened to the other man?' Mike asked.

'He's gone. I gave him the one million baht and he left,' Kung explained matter-of-factly. 'Now I just want to sell this guesthouse and leave this island so that he can't find me ever again.'

Mike rented a scooter in Phuket and started to explore the island on his own. The more he saw of the island, the more he liked it. Phuket is Thailand's largest island, so there is a lot to discover beyond Patong. One day by chance, Mike stumbled upon a beautiful place called Karen beach. It was a tourist area with a lot of farangs, but it wasn't nearly as developed as Patong. The next day Mike moved all his stuff to a hotel by Karen beach. Mike had stayed in super touristy areas such as Pattaya, Chaweng Beach in Koh Samui and Patong in Phuket, but Karen Beach was different to those places. It was much quieter and more laid-back. He thought it would be a perfect place for him to settle down again.

Faith is a strange thing. One week after he moved to Karen Beach, Mike was enjoying a late breakfast in a restaurant by the beach when he heard a middle-aged Australian couple at the next table arguing about money. From what Mike could gather, they owned a business in Karen Beach, but it wasn't making enough money to pay off their loans so they wanted to sell up and go back to Australia. Mike's curiosity got the better of him, and when the argument died down he apologized for interrupting their breakfast and said, 'May I ask, what kind of business do you own?'

'We own a hotel near here,' the Aussie woman replied.

'After you have finished your meal, could you bring me to

have a look at it?' Mike asked, spontaneously.

After they had all finished their meals, the Australian couple brought Mike to have a look at their hotel. It was a ten-bedroom hotel about one hundred meters in from the beach. There was a penthouse on the top floor, and behind the penthouse there was a beautiful, spacious apartment in which the owners lived. The hotel looked modern. Everything was immaculate – both the interior and the exterior. Mike was impressed.

'How is business?' Mike asked.

'It's quite good,' the man said confidently. 'We have bookings throughout the year, including low season. If it wasn't for the mortgage repayments, we would be able to live very comfortably.'

'What's the asking price?'

'Ten million baht,' the woman answered without hesitation.

Mike agreed that the hotel was probably worth ten million baht, but he didn't say that to the couple. Instead, he stroked his chin, deep in thought, and said, 'That's a bit out of my price range.'

'Look, it's like this,' the husband said, 'we'd love to get out of debt and go home. We were hoping for ten million, but make us an offer and we'll see what we can do.'

Mike loved the hotel. He thought it would be a great business to have. Mike told the couple that he was interested but he needed some time to think it over.

The following week, Mike got a call from Kung. She said the

sale of the guesthouse had gone through without any problems.

'I am coming to Phuket,' she said.

The next day, Kung walked into Mike's hotel room with all her stuff and wrapped her arms around him like nothing had happened. Mike welcomed her warmly. He had missed her terribly since he came to Phuket. By the end of the day they were officially a couple again, and the next morning Mike brought Kung to see the hotel. Kung couldn't believe it. After everything that had happened, here was Mike showing her a new business opportunity for them to invest in together. Kung loved the hotel from the start. Mike and Kung agreed to offer the couple seven million baht. The couple quickly refused the offer.

'We can't afford to lose that much money,' they said.

Kung led the negotiations and she stood firm on seven million baht.

'Seven million is all we can afford, she insisted, knowing that the couple were desperate to sell. 'Please call us if you reconsider.'

A few days later the Australian couple came back to Mike and Kung. They said the lowest they could go would be 7.25 million baht, but they would include their old car and four scooters in the sale.

Mike and Kung were delighted. They used a lawyer in Patong to deal with all the paperwork. Mike paid five million baht and Kung paid the rest. Within a month the sale went through and they moved into the hotel.

Mike and Kung didn't need to make any changes to the hotel, and they even kept on all the same staff, so the place practically ran itself. They made a healthy profit each month because they didn't have a mortgage to pay off. Mike and Kung's relationship was stronger than it had ever been. They were able to spend a lot of time together away from the hotel. They enjoyed the peaceful atmosphere around Karen Beach, and they enjoyed getting in their car and driving around the island during the day. Mike felt fortunate that he had given Kung the second chance that she deserved.

About eight months after they bought the hotel, Mike needed to renew his passport. He wanted to go back to America to renew it. He thought it would be a good chance for Kung to see his country, but Kung didn't want to go.

'I can't leave the business,' Kung said. 'We are still in our first year and high season is coming.'

Kung insisted that Mike should go home for one month to sort out his new passport and catch up with friends and family. A few weeks later Mike flew back to America. He had a nice time back in his home country, while he waited for his new passport to be issued. He talked with Kung on the phone every day, but a few days before Mike was due to fly back to Thailand, Kung suddenly stopped answering her phone. Mike emailed her, but she didn't reply. During his last day in America, Mike tried to call Kung several times, but now her phone was switched off. Kung knew the date and time that Mike would arrive in Phuket Airport, but she was not there to welcome him. Mike got a taxi straight to the hotel. When he walked into the hotel, the first thing he noticed was that there was a new receptionist. Mike introduced himself, and then when he tried to walk past the reception to the elevator, the new worker stopped him.

Mike laughed and said, 'You don't understand. I am the owner.'

He tried to walk past her again, but she stopped him. Her English was not very good.

'Call Kung,' Mike said. 'Call the boss. She is my girlfriend.'

The receptionist went back to the desk to use the phone. A few moments later, the elevator opened and a nicely dressed woman in her fifties came out.

'Hello, sir. Who are you?' the woman asked Mike.

Mike thought she was a guest at the hotel, so he was surprised by her question.

'I'm Mike. This is my hotel. Who are you?'

'Oh, yes, I see. You are Mike,' she said, and then she spoke Thai to the receptionist.

The receptionist took a key from a small drawer and handed it to the woman.

'Mike, I bought this hotel two weeks ago,' the woman announced, very business-like.

'What are you talking about?' Mike asked, completely disorientated all of a sudden. 'I didn't sell the hotel.'

The whole situation felt surreal. Something was wrong. Nothing made sense. He had a hundred questions spinning around his head. Mike took out his phone and tried to call Kung again.

'I bought this hotel two weeks ago,' the woman explained again, not showing any sympathy or consideration towards Mike. 'I used lawyers and everything is official. I paid the money already.'

Kung's phone was still turned off.

'No, no. There must be some mistake.' Mike shook his head, bewildered. 'This is my hotel.'

'There's no mistake,' the woman replied, coldly.

That's impossible, Mike thought, this hotel belongs to me and Kung. There's no way you could have bought the hotel, unless ... unless Kung sold it without telling him. Is that why she stopped answering my calls and turned off her phone?

'Kung sold you the hotel?' Mike asked, now thinking more clearly.

'Yes.'

'How much did you pay?'

The woman was surprised by this question. She hesitated for a moment, but eventually she said, 'I bought it for 9.5 million. Kung wanted a quick sale.'

'Where is Kung?' Mike asked.

'I don't know. She sold the hotel to me and then she left.'

Mike went into a rant about how Kung had no right to sell the hotel without his permission. The woman didn't care about Mike's woes. She handed him the key to his car and asked him to leave.

'Not my problem, not my problem,' she kept saying, as she ushered him out the door.

Mike found himself standing in front of the hotel with his car key and his luggage from his American trip. His head was all over the place. He felt alone, abandoned, tricked, deceived, betrayed and belittled. He stood outside the hotel for a few moments, unable to move or think straight. The last time he felt this way was when he found Kung in bed with that man. It took a few minutes, but eventually Mike got a grip of himself again. He found his car in the car park, and when he opened the trunk he saw a big bag with all his stuff. He threw his luggage into the back seat and then he sat in the driver's seat while he thought about what to do next. Lawyers and police came to mind, but first he took a moment to consider the money involved. They had bought the hotel for 7.25 million baht, and Mike had paid 5 million of that. Kung had made more than two million baht profit on the sale.

Mike noticed something on the passenger seat next to him. It was his bankbook with a note on top. He read the note out loud: 'Mike, I'm sorry. You're special. I love you. Kung.'

Mike was devastated. He felt foolish for letting Kung trick him twice. He started the car and drove to Patong to see his lawyer, in the hope that he would be able to shed some light on this crazy situation. Annoyingly, the law firm was closed for lunch. Mike had an hour to kill, so he decided to grab his bankbook and go check his balance. He had 800,000 baht in that bank account; he was worried that while he was in America, Kung might have somehow accessed his account and withdrawn all his money. He went to a local bank and placed the bankbook into the machine. It updated the book and gave it back to Mike. He was expecting to see 'Balance: 0 baht' when he opened the bankbook, but when Mike read his balance, he couldn't believe his eyes. It didn't make any sense.

'That can't be right,' he said out loud.

Mike went into the bank and asked the bank teller to check his balance. He didn't trust the machine. The bank teller checked Mike's account and printed the balance on a small bank slip.

Mike took the bank slip and read 'Balance: 10.3 million baht'.

Kung had put all the money from the sale of the hotel into his bank account, and only he had access to that account. He couldn't believe it. Why would she do that? He kept asking himself, as he left the bank.

When the lawyer's office opened after lunch, Mike asked his lawyer to explain what had happened while he was in America.

'Kung came and arranged the sale,' he explained. 'The hotel was in her name and you got all the money, so we were able to put the sale through.'

The lawyer couldn't tell Mike much more than that.

'Did Kung seem okay?' Mike asked.

'Yes, she seemed in a bit of a rush to get the sale done, but apart from that she seemed fine.'

'Her phone is turned off. Do you have any way of contacting her?'

Mike realized that this lawyer might be the last remaining link between him and Kung.

'I'm sorry, Mike, she didn't leave a forwarding address,' the lawyer replied, sympathetically.

'Do you have a copy of her ID?' Mike asked, desperate for some scrap of information that might help him track her down.

'No, sorry.'

There was nothing more the lawyer could do for Mike.

As soon as Mike left the lawyer's office, he gave me a call. He explained that Kung had sold the hotel while he was in America, deposited all the money in his account, and then disappeared.

'That's the weirdest thing I've ever heard,' I said. 'Something must have happened to her. You must find her.'

Mike agreed. He started to think that perhaps the bad man from her past had somehow found her and started blackmailing her again. Maybe he threatened her or hurt her. Perhaps he took her away somewhere, or maybe she had to run away. These terrible ideas were suddenly running through Mike's mind. These terrible theories about Kung's disappearance were the only way to explain why she would give Mike all that money and then cut off all contact with him. Something bad must have happened to her, Mike thought. He didn't care about the hotel or the money; he just wanted to find Kung and make sure she was safe.

After he spoke to me on the phone, Mike rushed to the local police office, but they couldn't help him because Kung had done nothing wrong and Mike didn't even have a copy of her ID card. Next, he went to dozens of restaurants and cafés around Patong beach and Karen beach that Kung liked, and he asked the staff if they had seen her recently, but they all said they hadn't seen her in over a month. Mike booked into a hotel by Karen beach and as he lay awake in bed that night, he realized that he must somehow get a copy of Kung's ID card if he was to have any hope of finding her again. He wracked his brain trying to think of when he last saw Kung use her ID card. He remembered the time they rented two scooters on Koh Samui a couple of years ago. The scooter rental store copied Kung's ID card that day.

Mike didn't get a wink of sleep that night. He checked out of his hotel early and got a bus to Surat Thani, and then he took a ferry from Surat Thani port to Koh Samui. He knew this was a long shot. The scooter rental shop could have closed down. The owners could have changed. They might not keep copies of ID cards for long, and even if they have a copy of Kung's ID card, they might refuse to hand it over to Mike. There was so much that could go wrong, but it was the only piece of hope that Mike had left. When Mike's taxi pulled up outside the scooter rental store, he was glad to see that it was still open. He explained to the owner that he wanted to get a copy of his girlfriend's ID card and that he was willing to pay a thousand baht for it. Mike gave Kung's name and told him the rough dates of when she hired the scooters. Fortunately for Mike, the owner of the store was able to find a copy of Kung's ID card. It was an amazing stroke of luck, and it gave Mike renewed hope that he would be able to find Kung.

Mike went to the local police station and explained the situation to a police officer who could speak English. Mike handed him Kung's ID card and the police officer agreed to check the system. The police officer told Mike that Kung didn't have any criminal record, and there wasn't any indication where she was or that anything was wrong. Mike was devastated to find himself back at square one, but he was glad that Kung seemed to be still alive. Mike spent the next three months pounding the streets of Phuket, Samui and Pattaya with a photo of Kung, asking workers in bars, restaurants, cafes, guesthouses and hotels if they had seen her, but to no avail. He exhausted every avenue but he couldn't find her; there was no trail. Mike ended up back in Pattaya, renting a condo on a month-to-month basis. There was a big hole in Mike's life and he didn't know what to do with himself. He was lonely without Kung, and the pain of not knowing what happened to her followed him everywhere. Every time he walked along Beach Road he remembered the time they first met and the beautiful dresses she used to wear.

One year later, Mike got a call from his lawyer in Patong, Phuket. By now, Mike had given up looking for Kung. He resigned himself to the idea that he would never know the truth about what had happened to Kung. The lawyer told Mike that a lawyer in Trang (in the south of Thailand, near Malaysia) had been trying to contact Mike for the last couple of months.

'Is this about Kung?' Mike asked.

'Yes, Kung passed away a few months ago,' the lawyer said slowly.

Mike's heart sank.

'How did she die?'

'She died of a hereditary disease. The lawyer wants you to go to Trang so he can read you Kung's will. He was the lawyer of Kung's family since she was a little girl.'

Mike decided to go to Trang, with the hope of finally finding out what had happened to Kung.

Mike's lawyer agreed to go to Trang with him. They checked into the same hotel and went straight to the office of Kung's lawyer. The lawyer started to read the will methodically. Everything about the will seemed normal until the last part, when the lawyer read that Kung had left Mike a condo in Pattaya. Mike was blown away. He had no idea that she had a condo in Pattaya.

How could she afford a condo in Pattaya? He thought. But this was not the right time to think about money or property. Mike sat forward in his chair and suddenly started bombarding the lawyer with questions.

'What kind of disease did Kung die of?'

'I'm sorry, but Kung wanted that to remain confidential,' the lawyer replied, composed.

'How long did she have the disease?'

'I'm not sure.'

'Did she suffer? Did she die alone?'

'I'm not sure.'

'How could she afford a condo in Pattaya? Does she have any family?'

'I'm sorry. I cannot say anything. It is all confidential.'

Mike could see that he wasn't getting anywhere with this lawyer. He leant over to his lawyer and whispered to him, 'I will go back to the hotel. Please find out everything you can about Kung and what happened to her. Give him this.'

Mike handed him 20,000 baht to grease the wheels.

Mike went back to the hotel and waited in the lobby. An hour later, his lawyer came back and sat with him. The lawyer took a deep breath and started:

'A couple of weeks before Kung sold the hotel, she got a call from her sister-in-law, her brother's wife. They had not spoken for a long time, so this call was completely out of the blue. The sister-in-law told Kung that her brother was dying and that she should come quickly to say goodbye before it was too late.'

'I thought Kung's brother died a long time ago in a car crash,' Mike interrupted.

'No,' the lawyer said. 'Kung only ever had one brother and he died just over a year ago of a hereditary disease. Kung and her brother did not have a good relationship, so they didn't contact each other for a long time, but Kung was lucky that she was able to see her brother one last time a couple of hours before he passed away. After that, Kung got tested for the hereditary disease too and the results were not good. The doctor told her that she had less than a year to live.'

'What disease?' Mike asked.

'I don't know. Her lawyer would not tell me the disease, no matter how much I pushed him. She didn't want to burden you with having to take care of her. She didn't want to put you through all that, so she sold the hotel quickly and moved to Trang.'

'Did she die alone?'

'No, she stayed in her old family home in Trang with her sister-in-law.'

'And the condo? How could she afford that? I thought she didn't have much money.'

'She had money,' the lawyer said. 'She came from a very wealthy family, more than you can imagine.'

Mike was stunned. Kung came from a wealthy family. She

kept that quiet. Mike was saddened that Kung had not let him take care of her in her time of need. He loved her and would have stayed by her side until the very end. But Mike was still confused. If her brother didn't die in a car crash, whom was that man he caught Kung with in bed? Mike never found out the answer to this question, but he never let it taint the memory of his lovely Kung.

Mike decided to stay in Pattaya. He moved into the condo that he inherited from Kung, and he tried to get on with his life one day at a time. Mike will always remember the day he first saw Kung on Beach Road. As she was leaning against a tree, she turned around, smiled at him and hooked him. Mike's life changed forever that day. Kung disrupted the peaceful retirement that he had long been looking forward to, and her disappearance broke his heart, but Mike has great memories of Kung to keep him warm at night. Mike's story is a sad one, but it shows that there are good people out there, even on Beach Road, Pattaya.

Illusions and Confusion

A couple of months after I started working as a bar manager in Pattaya, an old Irish mate of mine called Craig visited Thailand for two weeks. He checked into a decent hotel on Second Road and headed straight for my bar to catch up with me, and probably to get a free beer. It was great to see an old friend again. I gave him a couple of beers on the house and we chatted for hours at the bar. He thought it was hilarious that I was working as a bar manager in Pattaya.

'Simon, I never knew you wanted to get into this line of work,' he said.

'Nor did I,' I said. 'It wasn't planned. It just kind of happened.'

That night Craig went back to his hotel room because he was tired from his long journey and probably a bit jetlagged. He came to my bar the next few nights, but he always left early. Craig enjoyed flirting with the girls in my bar and he bought several of them lady drinks, but he never barfined any of them. They didn't seem to be his type. Instead, Craig left my bar when the night was still young and went looking for girls in other bars. This story starts on Craig's fourth night in Pattaya, after he picked up a freelancer on Beach Road and brought her back to his room.

As soon as the freelancer left his hotel room, Craig hurried to check his wallet, his credit cards, his phone and his camera. Good, everything was still there. Craig had been coming to Pattaya twice a year for the past eight years, but this was only his fourth or fifth time going with a freelancer. He had heard a lot of stories about how they rob your stuff or refuse to leave your room until you give them extra money for a taxi home. Craig was relieved that his experience with a freelancer passed without any problems. It was only 10 pm, so he had a quick shower and headed out for more action.

Although it was the fourth night of Craig's trip, he had not yet stepped foot on Walking Street, so that's where he decided to go for a few beers. It was low-season and it was still early in the night, so Walking Street was not as hectic as he remembered it. Having said that, there were still people constantly trying to get his attention and drag him into go-go bars, ladyboy bars, bars with Russian women and countless other bars and clubs promising cheap beer. Craig passed a bar with only three working girls and no customers. He figured it would be a good place to have a quiet beer and enjoy watching the crazy scenes on Walking Street. Craig ordered a beer and sat at a stool looking out over the street.

When one of the girls brought Craig his beer, she sat on the stool next to him and asked: 'One lady drink for me?'

'No, sorry. I just want to drink alone,' he said, as kindly as he could.

Craig had just been with a woman, so he had no interest in going with another woman so early in the night. He just wanted to sit alone and enjoy a few beers.

'No problem,' she said, but then two minutes later one of the other girls came over to him.

She made small talk with Craig for a few minutes and then asked him to buy her a lady drink.

Again, Craig made it clear that he wanted to be alone. The girl left Craig alone but she seemed annoyed. Craig finished his first beer in peace. He ordered another beer, and this time the third girl brought it to him. She sat next to him and tried to turn on her charm.

'You look so handsome,' she said. 'Why handsome man like you alone?'

She kept talking for a couple of minutes and then she asked Craig to buy her a lady drink.

'No,' he said, this time a little firmly. 'I really just want to be alone.'

These girls weren't to know that Craig had just finished with a girl forty minutes earlier. They probably just thought he was being a cheap Charlie.

Now that Craig had refused all three of the girls, he thought surely he will be left alone to enjoy his second beer. But things started to get a bit weird and uncomfortable. The girls were sitting at the bar behind him. They were chatting to each other in Thai and they kept saying something-something 'farang', and when Craig turned around to look at them, they burst out laughing. Craig sensed that they were taking the piss out of him. He suddenly felt like a fool in that bar with those girls, so he paid his bill and walked out. There were plenty of other bars around.

Craig was pissed off about what had just happened, so he left Walking Street and headed towards the beach. He walked along Beach Road to clear his head. It would have been a nice walk along the side of the beach if it wasn't for all the ladyboys propositioning him. After about fifteen minutes, Craig spotted a nice bar across the road. He sat at a stool facing the beach and ordered a beer. The girl who brought Craig's beer seemed quite a bit older than the other girls. She looked like she was in her late thirties, but she was very pretty and had a curvy body. She sat down alongside Craig and said: 'My name Nit.'

'My name is Craig, but I really just want to be alone. Sorry.'

'No problem,' Nit said, with a great kindness in her voice. 'Many customer want to be alone. I understand.'

Nit left Craig alone to drink his beer and enjoy the view of the white waves crashing against the night beach. But he kept his eye on Nit too. He thought she looked like a genuinely kind and friendly person by the way she spoke with the customers and the other girls in the bar. The other girls were taller and sexier, but they looked cold and arrogant compared to Nit.

When Nit brought Craig his second beer, she asked if he would like to play pool with her. Craig was surprised. He hadn't noticed that there was a pool table in the back corner of the bar. Craig loved pool, so he agreed to give Nit a game. As they were playing, Nit managed to get a lot of information out of Craig. She found out that he was from Ireland, he was in his mid-forties, divorced, and he was a lorry driver. Craig also told Nit that he was a regular to Pattaya, and this was his fourth day of a two-week trip. Craig won two games of pool, but Nit was a decent player. She must have played a lot.

Craig went back to his stool facing the beach. A few minutes later, he was surprised to see Nit leave the bar and walk down the road. There was a bathroom near the pool table, so he couldn't understand why she would just leave the bar suddenly. Five minutes later Nit came back with a small bag of sliced pineapples. Nit placed her hand on the stool next to Craig and said, 'Can I sit here? We eat together.'

Craig and Nit chatted away while they ate the pineapple slices. They got along very well. Nit was very easygoing and she never asked Craig to buy her a lady drink. When the pineapple slices were finished, Nit stayed to chat with Craig some more. They were having a lovely time together. After half an hour Craig asked Nit if she would like a drink. She accepted. They had a few drinks together and a couple more games of pool. Craig was planning on having a quiet night on his own, but Nit was lovely.

He didn't want to miss his chance with her, so towards the end of the night, he paid Nit's bar fine and brought her back to his room. They jumped into the shower and Nit washed him all over, up and down, in a very sensual way. It made quite an impression on Craig. She was a very warm and attentive woman. They had their fun and an hour later Nit left with a thousand baht in her pocket.

The next day Craig went back to the bar to see Nit, only this time he barfined her and asked her to spend the whole day with him. Craig enjoyed Nit's company. She seemed completely different to the other bargirls he had met over the years. Craig wanted to go shopping, so Nit brought him to some cheap stores that he had never been to before. In the evening she introduced him to some nice Thai street food. He really enjoyed spending time with Nit. Not only was she beautiful and kind, but she was also teaching Craig a lot about Thailand. At night, they had a few drinks in a very quiet bar by the beach, and Craig asked Nit some personal questions. He was surprised to hear that she had no family. She didn't have any siblings and both her parents had died when she was young. Nit didn't own any house or land in her old village. The only place she called home was the small room she rented in Pattaya. She never got married and she didn't have any children. She was all alone in the world. When Craig heard Nit's story, he felt sorry for her. He wanted to take care of her.

That night, as they lay in bed together, Craig said to Nit: 'If I pay your bar fine, would you like to come down to Krabi with me?'

Craig suddenly wanted to explore other parts of Thailand, especially some of the islands down south. He didn't do it before because he was always on his own, but now he had Nit to accompany him.

'You like Krabi?' Nit asked, surprised that Craig suddenly talked about going on a trip.

'I've never been before,' he said, 'but I heard it's nice. Do you want to go with me?'

'Yes, I want, but I no have money,' Nit said, looking embarrassed.

'I will pay for everything. Don't worry about money. I just wanna get out of here. I'm sick of Pattaya.'

'But if I stay in bar I make good money everyday. If I go Krabi, I no make money.'

Craig knew that the bar paid Nit a salary, and she also got money from going with customers. So, to compensate Nit for her time, Craig said he would pay her one thousand baht per day. She didn't look overly pleased with this modest amount, but she agreed to go on the trip, probably with the hope that she would be able to squeeze more out of Craig along the way.

The next morning they went to Nit's bar together and Craig paid the mamasan 1500 baht to take Nit out of the bar for a week. On their way to the airport, Craig dropped by my bar and introduced me to Nit. She seemed kind of quiet and shy for a bargirl, but perhaps that is what Craig liked about her. I was surprised to hear that Craig had paid Nit's bar fine for a week and was bringing her to Krabi. It was completely out of character. He rarely spent more than one night with bargirls. I wanted to ask Craig about this, but Nit was right next to him the whole time and they were in a bit of rush to go to the airport.

They got an afternoon flight down to Krabi and found a nice three-star hotel by the beach in Ao Nang. After they checked in, they went outside for a walk around the area. There were a lot of small tour shops offering trips to all the small islands around Krabi. Craig looked forward to visiting some of the famous spots, like Phi Phi Island and Maya Beach. These tour shops also offered scuba diving courses and snorkelling day trips. Craig had never tried anything like that before, and he thought it would be a nice way to spend a day with Nit.

Ao Nang had a completely different vibe to Pattaya. There were some cheap guesthouses in the area, and there were a lot of young backpackers walking around. Craig had never seen this side of Thailand before – he loved it. With the chilled-out vibe and the beautiful ocean, it felt like paradise to Craig, and it was all the more perfect because Nit was by his side. In the evening, Craig and Nit went for dinner in one of the many seafood restaurants along the beach front, and then they moved on to a bar for a few drinks. Craig and Nit made a lovely couple. They were getting along great and their feelings for each other were growing rather than fading.

At about five o' clock in the morning, Craig was fast asleep when Nit started shaking him to wake him up. Craig half opened his left eye and looked up at Nit. She was fully dressed.

'I have to go,' she said, in a panic. 'My mom is sick. I need money.'

Craig was still half asleep and a little drunk; he didn't know what was going on.

'Quick! I need money, please,' Nit pleaded desperately.

Craig reached for his wallet on the bedside locker and took out his last three thousand baht in cash. He shoved the notes into Nit's hand and fell back asleep.

Shortly after eight o' clock, Craig woke up. When he saw that Nit's side of the bed was empty, he assumed that she was in the bathroom. It took him a few minutes to fully wake up and realize that there was no sound coming from the bathroom. He knocked on the bathroom door and called out 'Nit?', but there was no answer. He opened the door tentatively and found an empty bathroom. Where are all her toiletries? Craig wondered, and when he looked around the hotel room he found that all Nit's stuff – her clothes, her luggage, her make-up, everything – was gone. He sat down on the edge of the bed for a minute to wrap his head around this. He started to vaguely remember being woken up by Nit at some ungodly hour and being told that she had to go see her sick mom. So that wasn't a dream? Craig asked himself.

But Nit said her mom died a long time ago. This was all very confusing for Craig. He found his phone under his pillow and called Nit to get some answers.

'What's going on?' Craig asked as soon as Nit answered. 'Where are you?'

'Sorry. I on bus now. My mom sick, need to go home to take care her. No battery on phone. I call when I in home.'

'But you said your mom …' But before Craig could get the words out, the line went dead. Craig called her again straight away but her phone was off.

Craig went downstairs for breakfast. He called Nit several more times while he was eating, but her phone was still off. Craig couldn't figure out what was going on. He had been to Thailand many times and had spent time with dozens of Thai girls, but nothing like this had happened to him before. He was baffled by Nit's behaviour. Why would she lie about her mom being dead? He kept wondering. By the end of his breakfast, Craig concluded that Nit probably did have a mom. He knew that Nit was from Isan, way up in the northeast of Thailand, far from Krabi, so she probably wouldn't arrive home and turn her phone back on until tomorrow.

Craig was now alone in Krabi, and he had already paid for the next six nights in the hotel. He decided to stay in Krabi but he didn't enjoy himself. His trip was ruined. Nit didn't call Craig the next day or the day after that. He called Nit dozens of times during his six days in Krabi, but she still hadn't turned her phone back on. Craig spent most of his time in the hotel, occasionally going out for a walk along the beach and to get some food. He wasn't in the mood to visit other islands or to go snorkelling. At night he went out to have a few drinks in some bars along the beach, but he cut a lonely, miserable figure sipping beer with a depressed look on his face. He missed Nit and he was worried about her.

After Krabi, Craig flew up to Bangkok and got a taxi to Pattaya. He still had two days left before his flight home. Craig arrived in Pattaya in the late evening. He checked in to his regular hotel and headed straight to Nit's bar. Craig saw the mamasan sitting at the bar punching numbers into a calculator and writing in a little black notebook. She looked up when she noticed someone stop right next to her.

'You back?' she said, all smiles.

Craig explained that Nit had left suddenly on their second day in Krabi.

'Yes, Nit call me and tell me her mom is sick, so she go home to take care her mom. Very far. Her home is Nong Khai, near Laos.'

'But Nit told me her parents died a long time ago.'

The mamasan just shrugged her shoulders. It wasn't her business. To his left, Craig saw two of the bargirls whispering to each other. They looked over at Craig and started giggling together. It looked like they were laughing at him. Craig felt that something wasn't quite right about all this, but he couldn't put his finger on it.

'I paid a bar fine for a week, but she left on the second day,' Craig said to the mamasan, rather firmly. 'I should get a refund.'

'Yes, I understand you,' the mamasan said, seemingly sympathetic to Craig's troubles 'But you must talk with Nit. She give you money when she come back.'

'When will she come back?'

'Don't know. Sorry.'

Craig knew that none of this was the mamasan's fault, so he didn't push the issue.

Craig drank in my bar that night. He told me about how Nit had lied about not having a family and then having to leave suddenly to go take care of her sick mom. It sounded dodgy to me, but I didn't say anything. Craig drank with me until the early hours of the morning and then went back to his hotel room alone. He had no interest in meeting another woman.

On his last day in Thailand, Craig visited Nit's bar again. He handed the mamasan a piece of paper with his email address. 'Please tell Nit to email me,' he said, and a few hours later he left for the airport. The timing of it was amazing, but when Craig was in the airport, he was about to turn off his phone when he got a call. His face lit up and his heart started pounding with excitement when he looked down and saw 'Nit Calling' on his phone screen.

'Where you?' she asked.

'I'm in the airport. My flight is in forty minutes. Where are you?'

'I in home now. My mom leave hospital today,' Nit explained, sounding very sad. 'I take care her in home now. I'm so sorry I no see you before you go. When you come back Thailand?'

'Maybe in three months,' Craig replied, already moving some figures around in his head. 'Maybe sooner if I can afford it.'

Craig told Nit that he was delighted to hear from her and that he hoped her mom gets better soon.

'I gave the mamasan my email address for you, but I will send it to you now in message.'

'Yes, send me. I want email you,' she said, warmly, 'and when you come Pattaya again I want see you.'

After the call, Craig and Nit exchanged email addresses by SMS. Nit's call put Craig in a great mood for his flight back home. He felt more relaxed and optimistic about everything now that he knew that Nit was okay and he had a way of staying in contact with her.

Craig returned to Ireland and over the next few months he and Nit emailed each other a lot. Nit was very apologetic about leaving Craig alone in Krabi and for not telling him about her mom. Nit said all the right things in her emails to keep Craig interested. She said that she would make it up to him the next time he visits Thailand, and of course she ended every email by saying how much she missed Craig. But the thing that impressed Craig the most about Nit's emails was that she never asked him for money. Craig had heard countless stories about Thai women asking their farangs to send them money for any number of reasons. Nit was different to those women. Her mother had just come out of hospital, so she had the perfect chance to ask Craig to send money to help with the hospital fees and medication costs, yet she didn't ask him for anything. To Craig, this was clear proof that Nit was not like the other bargirls in Thailand. It proved that she was honest and independent. Craig couldn't wait to see her again.

Craig saved money quickly and within three months he was on a flight back to Thailand. He didn't tell Nit that he was coming. He wanted to turn up at her bar and surprise her. Craig's flight landed in Bangkok late at night, and by the time he arrived in Pattaya by taxi, most of the bars were already closed. Craig checked into his regular hotel. When he got into the elevator, he saw an old farang with a beautiful young Thai woman. They were holding hands, but from the way they were talking to each other, Craig could tell that they had only just met. She was probably either a freelancer who he had picked up on the street or a bargirl who he had bar fined. Either way, Craig was glad that those days were behind him. He felt much better coming to Thailand knowing that there was a beautiful, kind woman who would be thrilled to see him and genuinely delighted to spend time with him.

Craig woke up late the next day. On his way to Thailand, he had bought perfume in the duty free for Nit, so he grabbed the duty free bag and went downstairs for a bite to eat. While he was eating, he thought a lot about what he and Nit would do during this two-week trip in Thailand. He didn't want to stay in Pattaya the whole time. There were so many interesting places in Thailand that he had heard about but had never visited, such as Chiang Mai up north and Phuket down south. Now that he had a travel companion in Nit, Craig also thought it would be fun to spend some time in Bangkok. He had spent a few days in Bangkok with friends a few years back, but he liked the idea of exploring more of Bangkok with a Thai person. Craig was excited about this trip; it was a great chance for him to explore Thailand and see new things with a lovely woman by his side.

After his meal, Craig headed to Nit's bar on Beach Road. It was early in the afternoon so there was only one other customer – a farang. The mamasan seemed happy to see Craig.

'Is Nit here?' he asked.

'No, she not come work yet,' the mamasan replied. 'I call now.'

Craig ordered a beer from one of the girls while the mamasan called Nit.

The mamasan called Nit a few times but she couldn't get through.

'Nit no answer,' she told Craig. 'Better you come again later. I think she come to work 6 pm today.'

Even though Nit was not due at work until the evening, Craig decided to stay and have a few beers as he looked out on to the beach. He had nothing better to do. The mamasan continued trying to get through to Nit. Craig noticed that she seemed in a bit of a panic.

'Don't worry about it,' he told the mamasan. 'There's no rush.'

'You go and come back at 6 pm. Better for you,' she said to Craig.

'It's okay. I am happy having a few beers here. Don't worry.'

The mamasan kept calling Nit and she even sent one of the girls out to look for her. Craig sipped away on his cool beer and he struck up a conversation with the other farang on the other side of the bar. This farang was an American in his mid-fifties. His name was Luke and he was clearly a very wealthy guy. All his clothes were designer gear and he wore nice jewellery. He reeked of money.

Craig picked up his beer and moved to a seat closer to Luke. As it turned out, Luke also had a girlfriend working in this bar. She had just popped down the road to get some Thai food. Luke explained that he had been seeing his girlfriend for the past two years. He visited Thailand three or four times a year, and he usually went to stay in a five-star hotel in Phuket with her. Luke mentioned that his girlfriend was older than the other girls and that she was good at pool. It suddenly dawned on Craig that they might be waiting for the same girl.

'What's your girlfriend's name?' he asked Luke.

'Nit.'

'Fuck!'

Craig was devastated, whereas Luke just laughed.

'What did you expect?' he said to Craig. 'She's a bargirl. Of course she goes with other guys.'

'I know,' Craig said, 'but it still feels shit.'

A strange thought suddenly occurred to Craig and he started asking Luke about the dates of his recent trips. As it turned out, the day after Craig took Nit to Krabi on his last visit, Luke arrived in Phuket in the early morning. He assumed that Nit was in Pattaya, so he sent her money and told her to get the next flight down to Phuket.

'She arrived before lunch,' Luke said. 'I remember thinking at the time that she arrived much quicker than I expected.'

'That's because she came from Krabi that time, not Pattaya,' Craig said, fuming. 'She told me her mom was sick, asked me for money, and then went to stay with you.'

'I pay her a lot more than the going rate,' Luke explained. 'So that's probably why she left you that time. Don't take it personally.

It all boils down to money with these girls.'

Craig knew that Luke was right. Nit was a bargirl who probably went with a different customer every night. She wasn't his girlfriend. She didn't have any reason to be loyal to Craig over her other customers. Craig understood all this, but he still felt used and betrayed by her. He felt stupid for thinking that Nit was different to the other girls and for convincing himself that they had something special together.

While Craig was getting his head around the situation, Nit walked into the bar and her face dropped when she saw Luke and Craig sitting together. She stopped in her tracks, speechless. The mamasan said something to her in Thai, probably something along the lines of 'I tried to call you to warn you, but you didn't answer your phone.'

Craig walked over to Nit. He didn't shout at her or get aggressive, but his voice was definitely filled with anger when he said, 'I know what's going on. I know your mom wasn't sick. You left me in Krabi to go stay with him. Didn't you? How could you lie like that?'

Nit was being embarrassed in front of her colleagues. She was losing face because Craig confronted her, so, like Thai women tend to do when they lose face, she went into attack mode. Nit started roaring at Craig, calling him all the names under the sun. 'Crazy farang' and 'ding dong farang' were the two that she spurted out several times. This was a nasty side of Nit that Craig had never seen before. He was taken aback by her reaction. Now that Craig could see what kind of woman Nit really was, he didn't want anything more to do with her. He paid for his beer and walked away.

That night Craig didn't come to my bar. He just wanted to be alone so he drank beer in his room. By about 1 am Craig was a little drunk and he suddenly had the idea to email Nit. He had calmed down a lot and had taken time to think about the situation from Nit's point of view. Of course she had to lie to me, he thought, she is a poor girl who had a chance to earn more money from another farang. I can't blame her for that.

So, at around 1 am he sent Nit a simple email saying sorry for confronting her in the bar. Within ten minutes, Nit replied, saying that she was also sorry for her behaviour. She explained that Luke takes good care of her and pays her a lot of money, but she likes Craig more. These were just the words that Craig wanted to hear, and all of a sudden Craig's feelings for Nit came flooding back. Nit told Craig that she would be away with Luke for a week, but when she came back to Pattaya she would love to spend time with him. Craig agreed to wait for Nit. He drank in my bar every night for a week, but he never went with a woman. Then one afternoon he got a message from Nit saying: 'I'm back. Come to bar now.'

Craig's heart was jumping with excitement when he read the message. He rushed to the bar to see Nit. They started talking about how they would spend Craig's remaining week in Thailand.

I was bemused. In Pattaya there are more bargirls than farangs most of the time, so why would you bother sharing a girlfriend with another farang?

Craig never mentioned Luke again and never asked Nit about any of her other customers. It was an unspoken agreement that Nit had other farangs who visited Thailand regularly and spent time with her. They were kind of Nit's boyfriends, and now Craig was kind of her boyfriend too. He continued coming to Thailand every three months, and Nit continued giving him the girlfriend experience.

As far as I know, Craig still comes to Thailand regularly to meet Nit, but the difference is that now he has to work his schedule around Nit and her other boyfriends. I couldn't get my head around why Craig put up with this crazy arrangement, but he seemed happy, so each to their own.

Coming Up Short

I was nursing a terrible hangover the first time I met Matt. It was my second week as the manager of a new bar on Soi 7 in Pattaya. I was trying to keep my drinking to a minimum because it was such a new bar, but a group of lads from Ireland came to my bar and they were buying me beer all night. It would have been rude to refuse them. I had a thumping headache but I still managed to drag myself out of bed and go downstairs to open up at noon. I sat at the bar with a cup of coffee and a cigarette, watching the highlights of last night's football on the TV. The tomboy waitress was arranging the stock behind the bar. It was a Sunday so I didn't really expect any customers to come for a while, but then in walked a farang. This farang was vertically challenged; he must have only been about five foot. He ordered a coffee and sat at a chair facing the street. He seemed to enjoy watching the people pass by. When he finished his coffee, he brought his empty cup to the bar and asked for one more. This time he sat at the bar and introduced himself to me.

'I'm Matt,' he said. 'I just flew in a few hours ago.'

From his accent I could tell straight away that he was from England, somewhere down south.

'I'm Simon. Is it your first time in Thailand?' I asked him.

'No, I've been here loads – twice in the past year alone. I must have been to almost every bar on this Soi, but I don't recognize this place.'

'It just opened last week,' I told him.

'Are you the owner?'

'No, I'm the manager.'

Matt was forty years old. He was an outgoing and confident guy, and he was very easy to talk to. We talked for about half an hour over our coffees. He told me that he got divorced a few years ago and he was now renting a small flat back in England. He didn't have any kids so he was able to save his money and come to Thailand two or three times a year for a couple of weeks at a time. He was a self-employed lorry driver, so he could come and go as he pleased. Matt knew quite a bit about the bar scene and the bargirls in Pattaya. He had heard all the horror stories about the devious ways of Thai bargirls, and he boasted that he never fell for any of their tricks or games.

After his second coffee, Matt said that he liked the bar and would come back that night. Farangs often used to promise me they would come back later, come back tomorrow night, come back before they went back to their home country, but a lot of them never did. They probably intended to come back to my bar, but there are so many bars and bargirls in Pattaya that it is easy to be distracted. For example, in order for Matt to keep his promise and come back to my bar that night, he would have to pass dozens of bars and hundreds of girls on his short walk from his hotel to my bar. All it would take is one girl to catch his eye and drag him into her bar, and then his plan for the night, and perhaps his whole trip, would be completely changed. Newbies find it especially hard to stick to their plans in Pattaya because they are especially susceptible to the temptations of the bargirls. But, remember, Matt knew a lot about Pattaya and the bargirls. He wasn't likely to allow himself be dragged into random bars and be distracted by the working girls of Pattaya. So, as he promised, Mike came back to my bar that night. I was sitting in the corner arranging a playlist on my laptop, when Matt came up and shook my hand. It was still early, only about 8 pm, so there were more girls than customers. While Matt and I chatted, I could see the girls looking over at him. If he had sat down on his own, one of the girls would already have sat down with him, but because he came straight over and started chatting with me, they stood back. A few minutes later, Moi, one of the girls in my bar, came over to us and said, 'Simon, who your handsome friend?'

I introduced them both. I could see that Matt was instantly attracted to Moi. She was thirty years old and stood five foot eight – much taller than Matt. She had long jet-black hair down to her shoulders and her face was a little different to normal Thai women. To me, she looked half Chinese, but I never asked her about it. Whatever her roots were, she was beautiful and she was one of the most popular girls in the bar. I never said it to Matt, but I used to call Moi 'Ruth-less' because she would do anything to get ahead in life. Almost all the bargirls I knew had a stone heart when it came to dealings with their farang customers, but Moi was the worst of them.

Seeing that Matt had taken a liking to Moi, I left them alone to talk. He bought her a lady drink, and thirty minutes later he paid Moi's bar fine and took her back to his hotel room. He must have paid her for 'long time' and not 'short time' because she didn't come back to the bar again that night. They walked into the bar together the next day and Matt paid Moi's bar fine again. They stayed with each other for the rest of his two-week trip. I was surprised by this because usually farangs who frequently come to Pattaya don't stick with the first girl they barfine. The newbies do it a lot, but not the more experienced guys.

The day Matt was due to fly back to England, he came to have a coffee with me in the afternoon.

'I have completely fallen for Moi,' he said. 'She's great. She's so sweet and smart.'

Moi must have pressed all the right buttons in the last two weeks, I thought to myself.

Matt was an emotional mess on his last day. From our conversations over the previous few weeks, I learned that Matt hated his life back home. He was staying in a dingy flat, he didn't have much of a social life, and he was sick of his job. It broke his heart to have to leave Moi and go back to his life in the UK.

'When will you be back next?' I asked him.

'Not for a while, I'd say. I've been here three times in the past twelve months. I'll need to work for a while and then maybe come back again in about eight months.'

Moi brought Matt to the airport that afternoon, and then she was straight back working in the bar that evening. She was barfined by a Norwegian guy within an hour, around the same time Matt's flight took off.

Two weeks passed. One morning I was in the bar having a cup of coffee. A couple of the girls were there. To my surprise, Matt walked into the bar. Well, I was surprised but not surprised – so many farangs come back much sooner than planned.

'I didn't expect to see you so soon,' I said to him.

'I came back to surprise Moi,' he said, scanning the bar quickly. 'Is she here?'

'I have no idea,' I said, and that was the truth. I had just woken up and I had a terrible hangover.

The girls in my bar lived in a room upstairs, so I sent one of the girls up to check if Moi was there.

When the girl came back down, she said: 'Moi not there. She go for breakfast.'

I wondered if she was really having breakfast or if she was with a customer.

Matt sat with me for a while, in the hope that Moi would

come back from her breakfast soon.

'I thought you weren't coming back for eight months,' I said to him.

'I really like Moi,' he said. 'That's why I came back so quick. I can't really afford this trip, but it was horrible going back to work after I met Moi. I missed her so much.'

'Moi is a bargirl,' I told him straight. 'She has been a bargirl for a long time. She goes with customers for money. You told me the last time that you have been to Pattaya several times before and that you know the score, so I'm surprised to see you fall for Moi like this.'

He said, 'I know, but she is different.'

'Oh, she's different, is she?' I said, and I laughed because I had heard that one so many times before. 'She's special, is she?'

Matt knew I was teasing him, but he was a great one for banter so he took it well.

'She's older and more sensible than the other girls,' he said. 'I like being around her.'

'Look, mate,' I said. 'You've heard all the stories about farangs falling in love with bargirls and losing the shirt on their back, so just be careful, that's all I'm saying.'

'Yes, yes, I've heard all the stories,' he said, dismissively, 'but this is different.'

Moi didn't appear and she wasn't answering her phone, so Matt decided to go grab something to eat and come back to surprise her later. Shortly after he left, Moi appeared. As it turns out, she had been with a customer, and she was still wearing the clothes from the night before. One of the girls told Moi that Matt was back in town, so she hurried upstairs to get changed. She came back downstairs wearing one of her nicer, less revealing dresses. I often saw Moi wear that kind of dress when she was giving farangs the 'girlfriend experience'.

When Matt walked into the bar after lunch, Moi ran towards him excitedly and jumped into his arms like a woman truly in love. Matt was blown away by this welcome; he couldn't stop smiling. He had a quick drink with Moi in the bar, and then he paid her bar fine. Same as the last time, he paid her bar fine every day for two weeks. They spent all day, everyday together. They drank in various bars at night and they went around Pattaya during the day on Moi's scooter. The two weeks flew by, and on his last day he came to have a coffee with me again in my bar. Just like the last time, he was sad to leave Moi; he was almost in tears.

'I've fallen for Moi,' he said, sombrely. 'I know you think I'm crazy to fall for a bargirl, but Moi is different. She's a little bit older than the other girls. She's had enough of the bar scene and she just wants to settle down. I want to be the one she settles down with. I want to take care of her.'

'So what's your plan?' I asked.

'First, I have to go back to England and work for a while. I can't afford to come back here quickly, and I can't afford to give Moi money every month to stop working. I'll work straight for six to eight months and figure it out from there.'

Moi went with Matt to the airport in the taxi again, and she came straight back to work in the evening again. Matt had told her that he couldn't send her money every month, so you can't blame her for going back to work. Matt really did seem to be broke, so I figured I wouldn't see him for at least another six months, but three months later he turned up at my bar again. Moi was in the bar this time. She welcomed him with excited hugs and kisses. I gave Matt a beer on the house to welcome him back to Pattaya. I asked him about his plan for this trip. He said he wanted to take Moi to her village in Isan to meet her parents. He paid her bar fine for the week. They spent one night in Pattaya and the next day they got a bus to Isan.

Matt and Moi came back to the bar three days later, still looking very much in love.

'How did it go?' I asked, curious to hear Matt's first impressions of a rural Thai village.

'It was great,' he said, clearly touched by the experience. 'Her parents are very poor. They live in a small one-room building behind Moi's aunt's house. But they welcomed me and made me feel at home. They are lovely people. We've decided to get married.'

I almost laughed in his face.

'Married?' I said. 'You've only known each other for a few months.'

'I know, but we are in love.'

'But what are you going to do for money? I thought you were broke.'

'I'll work for a few months and when I come back we will get married. It will just be a small ceremony in her village.'

'And what will Moi do in the meantime?'

'I'll send Moi money every month so that she can leave the bar and go back to her village to prepare the ceremony.'

A few days later, Moi brought Matt to the airport. He gave her enough money to live comfortably for a month, plus a little extra for the bus fare back to her small village in Isan. He promised to send her more money in a month. Moi came straight back to our bar that evening. She had no intention of leaving the bar and going back to her village. She knew a wedding ceremony in a village could be organized in twenty-four hours if needed. But of course Moi told Matt that she was back in her family home and she accepted his money every month.

Matt returned to Thailand six months later, and they had a very modest ceremony in Moi's village. It was a Thai wedding ceremony but it didn't mean anything legally. To make it official they would have to go to the local registry office and register the wedding, but they put that off for another day. This wedding ceremony did not mean anything legally, but it was highly significant to both Matt and Moi. In Matt's eyes, he had married the woman he dearly loved, and in Moi's case she had gained face in front of the whole village by marrying a farang.

The night of the wedding, Matt told Moi that he wanted to bring her back to the UK to live. He figured she would be able to go to the UK on a six-month tourist visa or a fiancé visa. They decided to go to Bangkok the next day to start the process. Matt had all the documents prepared in advance. Matt and Moi went to the British embassy in Bangkok and submitted the application. They were told it would be a week before they got an answer. That worked out fine for Matt and Moi because they planned on going down south to Krabi for their honeymoon anyway.

During the honeymoon, Moi was in great spirits. She was excited about starting a new life in the UK with Matt. She asked him dozens of questions everyday about life in the UK, like what kind of job she would be able to get, what jobs paid good money, and about what options would be available to her if she wanted to study in a night school or college. She was determined to make the most of this opportunity.

Matt and Moi's honeymoon was cut a few days short when the British embassy called them and asked them to come for an interview. They got a flight back to Bangkok that evening. Both Matt and Moi dressed up nicely for the interview. They even went to a coffee shop before the interview so that Moi could practice answering some questions in English. They were both nervous but confident because they had nothing to hide. Moi was the first to be interviewed. It was very straightforward and much easier than she had expected. Matt's interview, on the other hand, was much more rigorous. He was asked in great detail about his financial situation, his job, and his intentions towards Moi. After the interviews, Matt and Moi waited around for an hour. Eventually their names were called and they were handed a letter. They were very excited as they opened the letter together, but when they opened it up, it read 'Visa request denied.'

Moi couldn't believe it. 'Why denied?' she asked Matt.

'I don't know,' he said, devastated. 'They don't really say.'

Matt knew that there were various reasons why the visa might have been denied. He didn't have any savings, he lived in rented accommodation, and as a self-employed lorry driver he didn't have any guaranteed income to prove that he would be able to provide for Moi in the UK. Matt explained these points to Moi very simply.

'So what we do now?' Moi asked, annoyed because Matt's promise of giving her a new life in the UK seemed impossible now.

'I can fix it,' Matt said, shaken by the setback but not defeated. 'I will go back home and fix this, I promise.'

'How?' Moi asked, unconvinced.

'I will go home and save money quickly,' Matt explained, his brain already running through different ways he might be able to get money together quickly, 'and then we can apply again. It can be fixed. Don't worry.'

However, the problem was that Matt didn't have any valuable assets to sell or close family to lend him large amounts of money. He was not at all convinced that he could fix this visa problem easily, but he didn't dare tell that to Moi.

At the airport Matt gave Moi enough money for two months and told her to go stay with her parents while he sorted out the visa problem. But Moi didn't go back to her village. She had just married a farang in front of the whole village, so she would lose face if she went back to the village alone to stay with her parents. So, she got a bus to Pattaya and came back to work at my bar, fresh from her honeymoon.

The lottery is incredibly popular in Thailand. Thai people of all ages go crazy for it. It is cheap and it gives people hope; it is a far bigger thing in Thailand than in any other country I have visited. But during all my time in Thailand, I only ever saw one person win serious money on the lottery. About three months after Matt went back to the UK, Moi won eight thousand pounds. It was incredible! Moi took me and all the workers in the bar for a nice meal that afternoon, and that evening she went back to work and carried on as normal – nobody ever mentioned the eight thousand pounds again. We all knew that we shouldn't mention it to any of Moi's customers, especially not to Matt. A couple of months after Moi's win on the lotto, Matt called her and told her that he couldn't figure out a way to bring her to the UK so he will come to live in Thailand instead. When Moi heard this, the first questions she asked were: 'How you come live here? You have big money?'

'Not yet,' he said over the phone, 'but I will. See you next month.'

Matt was desperate to start a new life with his new Thai wife. By the time he finally gave up on getting a visa for Moi, they had already been apart for five months. He couldn't take it anymore; it's no wonder that he started making stupid decisions. During his time back in England, Matt worked hard and he was able to save four thousand pounds. As soon as he decided to move to Thailand, he started selling all his stuff, for which he got about a thousand pounds to add to his savings. But Matt knew that five thousand pounds wouldn't last long in Thailand, so he went to the bank and he managed to secure a fifteen-thousand-pound loan. The interest on the loan was high, but it didn't matter because Matt had no intention of ever repaying it. In fact, he had no intention of ever setting foot on English soil again.

Matt now had twenty thousand pounds. He knew that customs only allowed passengers to bring ten thousand pounds on a flight, but Matt decided to bring the whole twenty thousand pounds in cash with him. He was lucky to get away with it. Moi met Matt at the airport and they got a taxi to a hotel in Sukhumvit. When they got to their room, Matt said: 'I have something to show you.'

He opened his bag and threw twenty thousand pounds in crisp bank notes onto the bed.

Moi's face dropped in shock, and then it lit up.

'How much?' she asked, now inspecting each bundle of notes to make sure the money was real.

'Twenty thousand pounds,' Matt replied proudly. 'But there is more where that came from. Tomorrow let's go to Chinatown.'

The next day Matt and Moi jumped in a taxi and headed to Chinatown. They went into the first gold shop they saw and Matt bought four thousand pounds worth of gold on one of his credit cards. Within an hour Matt bought a total of ten thousand pounds worth of gold on his three credit cards. They stopped to have lunch at a noodle stall, and then over the next couple of hours they went to ten different gold stores to sell all the gold for cash. He lost a couple of percent on each sale, but it was like free money to Matt because he had no intention of ever going back to the UK and paying off the cards.

Matt was on a tourist visa, so he wasn't sure if he could set up a bank account or not. Moi set up a bank account in her name and she gave the card and the bankbook to Matt. He put all the money into that account. Matt and Moi spent the next few days in Bangkok, and they used that time to consider and discuss what they should do next. The sensible thing would have been to rent a cheap room somewhere, make their marriage official and then sort out a marriage visa for Matt. Then, they could perhaps think about setting up a small business that could earn them a decent income every month. But Moi had different ideas. She was firm on the idea of buying land in her village and building a small house so that they would always have a roof over their head. Once they had a place to live, they could start to think about making money. Matt went along with Moi's idea. They bought some land near Moi's family and they got the local builders to build them a small house. It ended up costing Matt about ten thousand pounds altogether. Foreigners cannot own land in Thailand, so of course the house and the land were in Moi's name. Matt spent another five thousand pounds doing up the inside of the house, and then a further five thousand pounds on some furniture and two motorbikes for him and Moi. Before he knew it, Matt was down to ten thousand pounds.

Matt and Moi settled into village life. Moi dabbled in a few business ventures but she wasn't much of an entrepreneur and she never committed to any of her business ideas properly. Matt enjoyed the tranquillity of village life, but he got more and more stressed as his money dwindled away. After six months he was down to six thousand pounds. The problem was that he had no way of making money in Thailand. The only job for farangs that he knew of was teaching English, but Matt wasn't qualified for that kind of work.

One night after he had a few beers, Matt said to Moi: 'We need to do something quick. Do you think we can open a bar somewhere? Is it possible?'

'Maybe,' she said. 'But I don't know prices. We have to check. We can go Pattaya and ask Simon. He can give us advice.'

So, yes, a few days later Matt and Moi turned up at my bar in the afternoon. I was delighted to see both of them, but when Matt told me about what he had done with the fifteen-thousand-pound loan, the gold and the credit cards, I felt terrible. I couldn't believe he had been such a fool.

'I wish you had told me about all this at the time,' I said. 'I would have tried to talk you out of it.'

'What's done is done,' he said, not wanting to dwell on his obvious mistakes, because he must have dwelled on them enough while he was staying in the village. 'I'm looking to open a bar and I need your help.'

'How much money can you invest?' I asked, because that's all it came down to.

'About six thousand pounds.'

'No chance!' I said outright. 'That's not enough to open a bar. It's not enough to open any kind of business. You would need at least twice that amount.'

Matt was devastated. He had lost his last chance of making a life for him and Moi in Thailand. I felt bad for being the one who had to tell him, but I knew he needed to hear it straight.

It was sad to see Matt at such a low point in his life. I could see that he was afraid of his future and he was starting to panic.

My heart went out to him.

'The only advice I can give you is to go back to the UK and pay back your debts,' I said, and he nodded along solemnly because he knew it was the only path left for him to take.

Matt called Moi over to explain what I had told him.

'Simon said six thousand is not enough money to open a bar,' he explained. 'He thinks I should go home and pay back my debts.'

I suddenly remembered that Moi had won that eight thousand pounds on the lotto earlier in the year. If she added her winnings to Matt's money, they would probably be able to open up a bar. I watched Moi closely to see if she would take this moment to mention her lottery winnings to Matt, but of course she didn't. That was her money.

Matt and Moi left Pattaya a few days later. Matt didn't follow my advice. He went back to the village with Moi and stayed there for another six months until he was down to his last one thousand pounds. Eventually Moi ended up saying to Matt: 'There's nothing we can do now. It's time you go to your home.'

Matt used the last of his money to get a flight back to the UK. I can only imagine how difficult it must have been for him to leave his wife and go back to the UK to face his debt. Moi came back working in the bar. It had been a good year for her; as well as her win on the lotto, she also got a house, some land and a couple of motorbikes. Matt kept in contact with Moi for about six months, and then suddenly he stopped contacting her. We never heard from him again.

I learned from Matt that no matter how much you fall in love with a Thai woman, you should not try to settle down in Thailand unless you have all the finances in place. You either need a decent pension, huge savings or some way to get a steady income to live off. And even if your finances are in place, don't be in a hurry to go buying land and a house for your partner. I've seen and heard so many stories similar to this one. Farangs come to Thailand with limited savings in the bank, they fall in love, and a couple of years down the line they are penniless and alone. Rent first, sort out your visa, get to know your partner and the Thai culture more. Taking it slow is the only way you'll have a chance of having a lasting relationship in Thailand.

Filter the Search

Hans was a German factory worker in his early sixties and he was going through his second divorce, so his friends suggested he join them on a trip to Pattaya. Hans's divorce was dragging on and he needed to get away from it all. He had never been to the Land of Smiles, but his friends averaged two visits a year. They got a flight from Frankfurt to Bangkok, and from there they got a taxi straight to Pattaya. They checked into a three-star hotel, took a nap to get over the jetlag, and when all three of them woke up and showered, they went out for a late dinner. Over dinner, Hans's two friends kept talking about how easy it was to meet girls in Pattaya. 'Pattaya will help you forget about your wife,' one of them said. 'You'll be fighting the girls off with a stick.'

Hans had heard his friends talk like this since they booked their flights to Thailand, but he never understood what they meant by it.

'Thai girls like German men?' Hans had once asked them.

They both laughed at Hans when he asked this question.

'You'll see for yourself when we get there,' they said.

They thought it was hilarious that Hans didn't know anything about Pattaya. He didn't do any research, so he assumed it was just a normal beach resort, not too dissimilar to the ones you might find in the south of Spain.

During dinner, Hans looked at the other customers in the restaurant and he watched the people passing by outside. He saw a lot of western men with beautiful Thai girlfriends, and he thought how lovely they looked together. He wanted nothing more than to meet a nice Thai woman and spend time with her during his vacation. From what his friends had told him about Pattaya, it seemed like he would be able to find a partner easily.

After dinner, Hans's friend said to him 'Are you ready for Soi 7?'

'What's that?' Hans asked.

'I'll show you.'

When Hans turned onto Soi 7 with his two friends, he suddenly stopped in his tracks for a moment. The music wasn't particularly loud at that time, and the street wasn't especially crowded, but Hans was blown away by the amount of girls standing outside the bars trying to entice tourists inside. He didn't want to walk down the street. To Hans, Soi 7 looked like a gauntlet. It was intimidating.

'Come on. You'll love it,' one of his friends said, as he shoved Hans forward.

The street seemed to be lined on both sides with Thai women. Most of the women looked like they were in their late twenties or early thirties, but there were some older looking ones and there were some that looked no more than eighteen or nineteen. A lot of the girls wore skimpy denim shorts and revealing tops, but Hans noticed that most of the older ones wore dresses that really emphasized their large breasts. There was something for every taste, that's for sure. Hans soon realized that every time he looked at a girl, she would call out to him: 'Handsome man, where you from?', 'Cheap beer', 'Where you go?' or something along those lines. It made Hans feel terribly awkward, so he just stopped looking at them. He kept his head down and followed his friends.

All the bars looked very similar – open layout, brightly lit with pink and red lights, a pool table, a lot of women standing in the entrance. It was difficult for Hans and his friends to pick one. About halfway down Soi 7, a beautiful Thai woman stood right in front of Hans and his friends and told them her bar was running a 'Buy 2 beers get 1 free promotion'. The offer was too good to turn down. At this stage it was about 9 pm. They were the only customers in the bar, but there were seven beautiful Thai women. Hans could see straight away that his two friends loved being around these women. They enjoyed joking and flirting with them, and soon they were playing pool with them, leaving Hans sitting on his own at the bar. Coco, the youngest of the bargirls, approached Hans and asked him if he would like to play a game with her.

'A game? What kind of game?' he asked.

'Jenga,'she replied.

That's the last game Hans expected to see in a bar in Thailand.

'You want to play Jenga with me?'

'Yes,' Coco replied, and then she placed the Jenga set on top of the bar and they started playing.

'If I win, you buy me drink, okay?' Coco said.

'Sure.'

Hans thought it was strange that the girls played Jenga with customers in the bar, but it was kind of fun, and while they were playing he was able to talk with Coco quite comfortably.

'When you come to Pattaya?' Coco asked.

'Today.'

'You come today? You come Pattaya before?'

'No, this is my first time.'

'How long you stay for?'

'Two weeks.'

'This your first time in Pattaya bar?'

'Yes.'

'I think your friends come Pattaya bar many time before. They tell you everything about Pattaya bar?'

'No, they didn't tell me anything.'

'Okay. I tell you. If you like me, I can go with you. But first you must pay bar fine.'

'Bar fine? What's that?'

'You pay three hundred baht to the bar and I can leave the bar for the night and go with you. But you must pay me money too, one thousand baht for short time. You want?'

Hans wasn't ready for any of this. This kind of cold, calculated purchase of someone's time and body was not the kind of female interaction he was looking for.

Of course Coco won the game and Hans bought her a lady drink, but he told Coco that he didn't want to barfine her or any other woman. Coco seemed a little annoyed with Hans and she suddenly didn't look as friendly or as lovely as she did during their game of Jenga. Hans didn't want to waste any more of Coco's time so he told her that he was tired and wanted to go back to his room. When Hans told his friends that he was leaving, they were shocked.

'What's wrong? That girl you were talking to is stunning?' one of them said.

'I know, but I don't want to pay to be with a girl for an hour,' he said.

Hans left the bar and agreed to meet his two friends the next day for breakfast.

Hans walked to the end of Soi 7 and when he saw the beach he decided it would be nice to sit on the sand and look out over the ocean for a while. It was too early to go to bed. While Hans sat on the beach, he started to regret coming to Pattaya. He could see now that his friends only came to Pattaya to get drunk and sleep with a different girl every night. Hans had one secret that he never told any of his friends, and that is that he didn't like sex.

He enjoyed kissing, hugging and being close to a woman, but he didn't, or couldn't, enjoy intercourse. The problem was that he could not get, never mind maintain, an erection when he was with a woman. Instead, he enjoyed masturbation, and only through masturbation in a room on his own could he ejaculate. This was the sole cause of his first divorce, and it played a hand (excuse the pun) in his second divorce too. It is no wonder that Hans had no interest in barfining a woman and paying her a thousand baht for an hour. Pattaya was wasted on him!

Hans got back to his hotel shortly after 10 pm. He still felt wide awake so he went online and started searching for things to do and things to see in Pattaya. While he was reading about Pattaya on various blogs, he saw Thai dating websites mentioned a couple of times. According to these bloggers, the dating sites were free and it was a good way to meet Thai women. Hans set up a profile on one of the dating websites, uploaded a photo, wrote a quick self-introduction and started looking through the women's profiles. Within a few minutes he got a message from a beautiful Thai woman in her early thirties named Ting. Hans and Ting sent each other messages back and forth for about ten minutes, and then Ting offered to come over to his hotel. Hans was surprised that Ting was moving so quickly. She was beautiful and he wanted to see her in person, but then she requested two thousand baht for her time, and that put a dampener on things for Hans. He turned off his computer and went to bed, but he was still optimistic. From what he had read on the blogs, a lot of the women on those kinds of websites are only after money, but if you keep searching you can find a gem. Hans vowed to keep searching while he was in Pattaya.

The next morning Hans met his two friends for breakfast. They quizzed Hans about why he had left the bar early and why he didn't want to barfine any of the girls. Hans explained that he was looking for genuine companionship, not a bargirl. He told his friends about the Thai dating website he had joined, but his friends were cynical about the idea.

'Mate, some girls over here charge a short time rate, some a daily rate, and some make you think that they are going with you for free, but trust me, you will always end up paying in the end. After coming to Pattaya for nearly ten years, I have realized that it is cheaper and easier just to pay the hourly rate and move on.'

Hans promised to keep his friend's advice in mind, but he was still determined to find a nice woman through the dating site.

On the third or fourth night of Hans's trip, he came to my bar with his two friends. While his friends played pool and chatted with the girls, Hans sat at the bar alone. Several of the girls came over and tried to hold Hans's attention, but he just wasn't interested. He was always very polite and gentle towards the girls, but it was obvious that he had no intention of buying them lady drinks or taking them back to his hotel room. I started chatting with Hans and we got along very well. I told him that he could come to my bar and have a peaceful drink at the bar anytime. I assured him that the girls wouldn't bother him. Hans started coming to my bar almost every night after that – sometimes with his friends, sometimes on his own. He would sit at the bar with me and chat for a couple of hours, and then he would head back to his hotel room at about ten o' clock to go on the dating website.

Every night Hans spent hours chatting with women on the website, while his friends chatted with women in bars. Hans even met one woman in person and spent the whole day with her. They ate nice food together, they went shopping, and at night they went to listen to live music by the beach. They were getting along great and Hans thought he had found a keeper, but at the end of it all, this woman revealed to Hans that she expected to be paid two thousand baht a day for her time. She claimed that she was taking time off from her work to be with him, so she thought it was only fair that he compensate her. Hans was devastated. He paid her two thousand baht for the day and then never contacted her again.

The dating site, and the trip in general, was turning into a big let-down for Hans. All the women on the site only seemed to be interested in money. Towards the end of his two weeks in Pattaya, Hans started using the site less and less. He had all but given up on finding companionship on this trip. But then one evening, a very attractive fifty-year-old woman named Dang sent him a message and he felt encouraged again. Dang was from Kanchanaburi on the River Kwai, which is almost three hundred kilometres from Pattaya. She was divorced with one son, but he was all grown up already. Dang was closer to Hans's age than the other women he had chatted with on the site, so perhaps this was the reason they understood each other and got along so well.

When Hans told Dang that he was due to fly back to Germany in a couple of days, she seemed very disappointed, but she said she was willing to drive to Pattaya to spend time with Hans before he left. Hans desperately wanted to meet Dang, but he was worried that she would drive all the way to Pattaya and then suddenly start demanding money from him. To avoid this, Hans said to Dang straight: 'Some of the girls I spoke with on this site want to be paid for every day they spend with me, but that's not the kind of relationship I am looking for.'

To which Dang replied, 'I understand. I no want that kind of relationship too.'

All she asked of Hans was that he book a room in his hotel for her and pay for the fuel for her car. Hans thought that was a fair request, so he agreed.

The following evening Dang arrived at Hans's hotel. It must have been a long drive for her, but when she arrived, she looked beautiful in an elegant knee-length black dress. Dang had shoulder-length straight black hair, she wore light make up and she looked closer to forty than fifty. As soon as Hans saw Dang, he knew that she was girlfriend material. They went to a nearby restaurant for dinner. Hans told Dang that he was going through a second divorce and he was looking for a new partner to love. Dang explained that she had not been with a man in ten years, since her husband passed away. Hans and Dang slept in separate rooms that night, but they met for breakfast downstairs the following morning. Over breakfast, Dang started to ask Hans more questions about his divorce, hoping to get a better idea of his financial situation. Hans didn't mention exact sums of money with her, but he did say that he planned to retire next year and he was not yet sure how he wanted to spend his retirement.

'If you come to Thailand, perhaps we can live together,' Dang said, tongue in cheek. 'I live in a beautiful area and it is much cheaper than Pattaya. I think you will like it.'

Hans took this moment to tell Dang that he does not like sex. As soon as Hans said it, he felt relieved that he had gotten it off his chest so early in their relationship. Dang was surprised to hear Hans mention sex suddenly over breakfast, but she took it in her stride and said, 'No problem. Sex or no sex, no problem. I like you because you good man.'

Dang seemed to be very easygoing about everything, including sex. This was very important to Hans. Now that Hans knew that Dang was not put-off by his sexual problem, he could start to think about their bright future together.

The trip was a success after all. Hans found a beautiful Thai woman who was genuinely interested in him and not his money, and she even seemed okay with his sexual shortcomings. Hans was sad to say goodbye to Dang so soon, but they promised to keep in contact daily and Hans promised to come back to Thailand in a few months to see Dang, his girlfriend.

The next year was a very busy time for Hans. He visited Thailand twice to spend time with Dang, he sold his house, he finalized his divorce, and he retired from his factory job with a nice pension. It was a shock to his friends and family in Germany when Hans decided to move to Thailand to enjoy his retirement with Dang. After he had sold his house and finalized the divorce, Hans was left with about six million baht in the bank, and he had a pension of about two thousand euro a month on top of that. Hans knew that he had enough money to live very comfortably in Thailand. So, only a few weeks into his retirement, he flew to Thailand to start a new life.

With the help of Dang, Hans settled into life in Kanchanaburi very quickly. Dang owned her own house in Thailand. She lived there with her sister and sometimes her son visited from Bangkok. But when Hans came to Thailand she moved in with him, and her sister stayed alone and paid Dang rent. Hans and Dang found a nice condo in a gated community for eight thousand baht a month. Hans did not plan on spending much money during his first few months in Kanchanaburi, but as soon as he moved into the condo, he realized that he would need to loosen his purse strings to make his new home more comfortable. Hans decided to spend big on a thick German brand mattress so that he could get a decent night's sleep, and he also splashed out on two large TVs (one for the living room and one for the bedroom). Hans didn't want to watch TV on the floor so he bought a leather three-piece sofa set, and he didn't want to eat while sitting cross-legged on the floor, so he bought a dining table and chairs. All these purchases were within Hans' first week in Thailand. In the second week, he bought a big double-door American-style refrigerator and other bits and pieces for the condo. Hans had not expected to buy so much so soon, but he was relaxed about the spending because he figured it was only natural that he would need to buy a lot of stuff to set up a new home in a new country. The only purchase Hans really hesitated over was when Dang suggested buying a new car. Dang's car was old and on its last legs.

'I never thought about buying a car in Thailand,' Hans said. 'Most people use motorbikes.'

'Yes, motorbikes are good for short distances, but don't you want travel Thailand and see new places?' Dang asked.

'Yes, of course I do.'

'Then we need car.'

Of course Dang wanted to buy a brand new car. Around this time Hans gave me a call and we chatted about how he was settling into his new life in Thailand. When I heard about all his spending and his plan to buy a new car, I advised him that he would be better off buying a secondhand car and investing in health insurance for himself. Fortunately, he took my advice. Hans ended up forking out seven hundred thousand baht on a secondhand SUV, and he also joined a good health insurance plan. Within his first three or four weeks in Thailand, Hans had gone through almost a million baht.

One evening Hans and Dang were chatting over a bottle of wine in the living room. At this stage, they had been living together for about a month, but in that time sex was never mentioned. Perhaps it was the second glass of wine that gave Dang the courage to bring up the topic that night.

'Do you want to have sex tonight?' she asked suddenly.

Hans didn't want to reject Dang by simply saying 'no'. He was worried that a simple 'no' might sound too cold and definite, so instead he pulled an apologetic face and said, 'I'm sorry.'

Dang nudged closer to Hans, looked him in the eyes, and said, 'Please tell me about the problem. We never talked about it. I no understand.'

Hans could not explain the problem very well to Dang, because he didn't even fully understand the problem himself.

'I can masturbate when I am alone,' he said, 'but I cannot have sex.'

'I know that. You say before. But why?'

'I don't know. I have always been like that.'

'Can you masturbate when someone with you?'

'I don't know. I have never really tried.'

'You want try tonight?'

Hans pulled the same apologetic face again and said, 'Not tonight. Sorry.' He had experienced this kind of conversation dozens of times with ex-wives and ex-girlfriends. He knew that the woman always starts off supportive and understanding, but over time they usually became frustrated and start to question the whole relationship. Hans hoped this would not happen with Dang.

In truth, Dang was already getting frustrated. She had been patient for a month, but now she wanted to work through the problem together. When Hans first mentioned this problem to Dang in Pattaya, she probably thought it was a minor issue that they could overcome together. She was starting to realize that she had underestimated the severity of Hans's aversion towards sex.

'I just want you to be happy with me,' she said, looking defeated.

Hans took hold of both Dang's hands and said, 'I am happy with you. This is the happiest I have ever been in my life. I am in love with you and I love my new life in Thailand with you. Sex is just not important to me. It's not a part of my life, so please don't worry about it.'

Dang was still bemused by the whole situation, but she decided to drop the issue and come back to it in a few months.

After they bought the secondhand SUV, the spending frenzy

quietened down. For the next month Hans only spent money on essentials, like food, gas for the car and bills. Retirement in Thailand with Dang was everything that Hans had hoped it would be – cheap, interesting and relaxing. But during Hans's third month in Thailand, Dang surprised him when she said: 'I want to move house.'

'What? We have only been in this place a couple of months,' Hans said, completely taken aback.

'I know, but my sister want buy my house. She doesn't want to pay me rent anymore. She thinks it waste of money. She want buy my house one million baht.'

'Okay. So you can sell her the house if you want. But why do we need to move?'

'When I get one million baht, I want buy nice condo near here. It is bigger this condo, and that condo complex has gym and swimming pool.'

'How much is it?'

'Three million baht. I get loan from bank two million baht. We can live in condo and pay loan every month instead of rent.'

It was a good idea. Hans was paying eight thousand baht a month rent on the current condo, but if they moved into this new condo they could use that eight thousand baht to pay off a two-million baht mortgage. Hans was interested and Dang could read it on his face.

'Or you can pay one million baht too. We can own condo

together and we only need one million baht loan from bank,' Dang suggested.

Hans agreed that it was a good idea but he was reluctant to use more of his savings so early in his retirement. He agonized over it, and after a week he told Dang, 'Let's go see the condo, and if I like it, I will put one million towards it.'

Dang was delighted. They went to see the condo the next day and Hans loved it. The complex had beautiful gardens, a large pool and a very modern gym. Now that he was old and had a lot of time on his hands, Hans figured it would be great to have a pool and a gym on his doorstep. He could get fit again and it would be a productive way to spend a couple of hours every morning. Hans transferred a million baht from his German bank to his Thai bank account, and then he withdrew the whole lot in cash and handed it to Dang. It seemed easier to him that way. It never occurred to him that it would have been better to have transferred the million baht to Dang's account.

It only took about a month for Dang to secure the one million baht mortgage from the bank and buy the new condo. The condo was in Dang's name, but she arranged for a document to be drawn up to show that Hans had contributed one million baht to the purchase of it. Everything went perfectly. Both Hans and Dang loved their new home. Dang loved it because it was the most spacious and modern home she had ever lived in, and Hans loved it because he could go for a swim before breakfast every morning and the pool was also a good way to beat the afternoon heat. To celebrate moving into their new home, they invited Dang's sister Bee over for dinner one evening. Hans bought nice wine and Dang prepared Thai food for the dinner party. A few hours before Bee was due to arrive, Dang let Hans know that Bee's friend would be joining her. Hans assumed that it was a male friend, perhaps a boyfriend, but he was surprised when he opened the door and saw Bee accompanied by a tall, strikingly beautiful young woman.

'Hello, my name is Jasmine,' she said.

Hans gave Jasmine a quick look up and down as he shook her hand. She was wearing black high heels and a very slim-fitting, sexy red dress. With the high heels, Jasmine was about six feet tall. Jasmine had a very curvaceous body and every move she made seemed to emphasize her curves. When she shook Hans's hand, she leant slightly forward and her breasts looked huge. When she walked into the living room with Bee, her ass swayed from side to side. Hans couldn't take his eyes off Jasmine.

The two hosts and the two guests sat together and chatted over a pre-dinner glass of wine. While they were all chatting, Hans started to wonder whether Jasmine and Bee were just friends or whether there was more to their relationship. Jasmine looked about thirty and she was a stunner, whereas Bee was in her mid-forties and she was very plain looking. Dang asked Hans to help her set the table, so Hans took this opportunity to ask: 'Are Bee and Jasmine a couple?'

'I don't know,' Dang replied. 'Why you care?'

Dang looked annoyed. She must have seen Hans staring at Jasmine.

Bee could not speak a word of English, so over dinner Bee and Dang spoke a lot in Thai. Usually this would have made Hans feel left out, but fortunately for him Jasmine spoke good English and she was very eager to talk with him. They talked together a lot over dinner and it soon became clear to Hans that Jasmine was flirting with him, not through her words but through her body language. She didn't play footsy with him under the table or anything like that, but she had other ways to show that she was interested in him. Jasmine wore light pink lipstick on her very pouty lips, and often when Hans was looking at her, she would take a small spoonful of food and place it very slowly into her mouth, and then pull the spoon out very slowly, pulling her lower lip down with the spoon on the way out. It was very seductive, very sexy. It was a wonder nobody else noticed her doing it, but Hans certainly noticed it.

After dinner, they all had some more to drink in the living room and around 11 o' clock Bee and Jasmine stood up to leave. When Jasmine was saying goodbye to Hans, she shook his hand again and slipped him a small piece of paper. Hans instinctively kept the piece of paper hidden and put it into his pocket discreetly. As soon as Bee and Jasmine left, Hans rushed to the bathroom, locked the door behind him and took out the piece of paper. His heart pounded when he read the note. It read 'Call me, Jasmine' with her phone number underneath. This was all very exciting to Hans. He couldn't believe that such a young beautiful woman was interested him. He hid the piece of paper in his wallet and over the next few days he considered whether he should call her or not. In the end, he decided not to contact Jasmine. He figured it wasn't worth the risk. Hans knew that even if he met Jasmine secretly and brought her to a hotel, he wouldn't be able to do anything with her. He wouldn't be able to perform. Instead, Hans started to think about Jasmine every time he masturbated. That was enough for him. He thought about her beautiful pink lips, her unusually large breasts and her long legs. He had never seen such a sexy woman before.

In the meantime, Hans and Dang were enjoying their nice life together, but they were starting to argue over the most trivial of things. The problem was that Hans and Dang were together twenty-four hours a day. Neither of them had a job or a hobby that took them out of the house, so they were always around each other. Dang recognized the problem, and one day she said to Hans, 'Me and Bee have cousin in Chiang Rai. We go visit for three days. Is it okay?'

'Without me?' Hans asked, surprised at the prospect of being left on his own.

'Yes, we need time alone. I go this Friday and come back

Sunday night. Okay?'

Hans was not too happy about being left alone, but he didn't have much choice in the matter.

When Dang left on Friday morning, Hans found himself at a loose end. He didn't like being alone. The condo felt big and empty without Dang. Hans felt lonely without her. To pass the time, Hans went swimming, he watched TV, and he even studied a bit of Thai to impress Dang with when she came back. On Saturday night, Hans was in the living room watching soccer on the TV when he heard a knock on the door. It was a scary moment because it was dark outside and Hans wasn't expecting any visitors. He didn't even know anybody in the area. Hans walked quietly to the door and looked through the peephole. He was surprised to see Jasmine standing at the other side of the door. He opened the door quickly and greeted her. She was wearing the same red dress, the same black high heels and bright pink lipstick. Hans had fantasized over that exact image for the past few weeks.

'Is Bee here?' Jasmine asked.

'No, Bee and Dang went to Chiang Rai to visit their cousin. They will come back tomorrow night.'

'Oh, yes. I forgot,' Jasmine replied, and then there was an awkward silence.

Jasmine looked at Hans and said, 'I walked here, very far. I'm very thirsty. Can I have some water?'

'Of course, of course. Come in.'

Hans lead Jasmine into the kitchen and poured her a glass of water. They sat at the dining table and started chatting.

'You are very handsome man,' Jasmine said to Hans. 'Dang is very lucky woman.'

'Thank you,' Hans replied, very turned on. 'You are a very beautiful woman.'

'No, no,' Jasmine said, putting her hands up to her cheeks to suggest she was blushing. 'I a little fat these days.'

'No, you are very slim.'

Jasmine stood up and placed her hand on her very firm stomach.

'I think I a little fat now,' she said.

Hans looked at her beautiful body. Jasmine didn't mind Hans looking at her. If anything, she seemed to enjoy it.

'No, you are beautiful,' Hans said, very excited.

At this moment, Jasmine gave Hans a naughty look. They held eye contact as Jasmine stepped closer to Hans. She placed her hand gently on his cheek and moved it slowly down his neck and onto his shoulder.

'Do you like me?' she asked.

'Yes,' Hans replied, without the slightest hesitation, 'I like you a lot.'

Jasmine took his hand and led him to the bedroom. They kissed passionately and Hans rushed to take off her dress and fondle her breasts. He couldn't believe this was all happening so quickly. But everything was going surprisingly well; he was turned on and fully erect. He was about to have full sexual intercourse for the first time in decades. When Hans tried to take off Jasmine's panties, she stopped him and said, 'I am a ladyboy, you know?'

Of course she was a ladyboy. Anybody who has been to Thailand and knows the bar scene would be able to tell in a heartbeat that she was a ladyboy. She was a very beautiful ladyboy, but all the telltale signs were there. She was much taller than the average Thai woman, she had an Adam's apple, her hands and feet were bigger than normal, and her voice was unnaturally high. But Hans was clueless about all this. He had only been to Pattaya once, and he spent most of that trip in his hotel room looking for girls on a dating website. He had seen several ladyboys in Kanchanaburi, but they all looked like cross dressers. Hans had no idea that a ladyboy could look as beautiful and as convincing as Jasmine.

Hans was shocked when Jasmine revealed that she was a ladyboy, but he wasn't turned off by it. He never told me the exact details about what happened that night, but he did say that it was the best sex he ever had. He was able to maintain an erection throughout and he had an amazing time. It was like nothing he had ever experienced before. He fell asleep with Jasmine in his arms, exhausted.

In the morning, Hans was awoken by the sound of a door

closing. At first he thought it must be Jasmine sneaking out without saying goodbye, but then he turned to his left and saw Jasmine fast asleep at the other side of the bed. When he heard footsteps get louder and louder as they got closer, he knew that it must be Dang. He closed his eyes and thought, oh God! I'm about to be caught red handed with a ladyboy.

He heard Dang walk into the kitchen first.

'Hans. Hans. Are you awake?' He heard her call out.

There was no way out of this. He leant over Jasmine and shook her gently to wake her up.

Before Hans could tell Jasmine that his partner was back early from Chiang Rai, the bedroom door swung open and in walked Dang. Her eyes almost popped out of her head when she saw Hans in bed with a ladyboy. Jasmine grabbed her clothes and ran out, afraid and embarrassed, leaving Hans to face the music alone.

By now Dang's shock had faded and she was brimming with anger. She started roaring at Hans.

'What the fuck you do?' she screamed. 'I thought you good man but you do this? You fucker! How can you do this? She ladyboy. She my sister's friend.'

Dang sat at the edge of the bed and started crying. She started shouting at Hans in Thai. He had studied a bit of the language, but he didn't have a clue what she was saying. Hans sat beside Dang. He apologized repeatedly and he tried to put his arm around her to comfort her, but she pushed it away furiously.

'Don't touch me!' she screamed. 'You disgusting!'

They sat in silence for a quarter of an hour while Dang cried her heart out. She eventually calmed down and she started asking Hans about what had happened. Hans explained that he didn't plan any of this and that Jasmine had just turned up out of the blue.

'But she is a ladyboy,' Dang said. 'You like?'

'I didn't know she was a ladyboy when we started. Maybe I like, I don't know,' Hans admitted.

Hans was as confused by this situation as Dang.

'Did you have sex with her?' Dang asked.

'Yes.'

'You say to me you cannot have sex.'

'That's what I thought.'

'Maybe you can only have sex with ladyboy.'

Hans didn't reply. He knew that she might be right.

Dang didn't seem angry anymore. Sitting at the edge of the bed, staring down at the tiled bedroom floor, she said, 'Hans, you cheat on me. We finished now. Please leave my home. I no want to see you anymore.'

Hans restrained himself and decided not to respond to Dang. He knew that if he was to reply to her, the argument would suddenly escalate. He thought if he waited some more, Dang might change her mind.

'Please leave,' Dang said again, still looking down at the floor.

Five minutes passed. 'I told you to leave. Why you no go?' Dang said, now looking at Hans in the eyes.

Hans couldn't restrain himself anymore.

'Why do I have to go?' he asked. 'This is my house too, and I own everything in it. If one of us has to leave, it should be you.'

Hans was shaking when he said this to Dang because he thought it would make her furious. But Dang didn't get angry. Instead, she laughed.

'Why you think this your house?' Dang asked.

'I paid one million baht towards this apartment.'

'No you didn't,' she replied, her face now void of any emotion.

Hans was surprised to see Dang talking like this.

'I did pay a million baht. You know I did. I have a document to prove I did.'

'That document not from lawyer,' Dang laughed. 'My sister make that document. It not mean anything.'

Hans was starting to panic now.

'The furniture is mine. I bought almost everything in this place,' he yelled.

'No, you didn't,' Dang said, still very calm, making it look like an adult talking to a petulant child. 'You give me cash as present and I buy this furniture with it. It's mine.'

Hans was in shock. He was speechless.

Dang went into the bathroom. Hans remained seated at the

edge of his bed, his head spinning. When Dang came back, her attitude was not as calm as before.

'Why you still here?' she said, annoyed, as if Hans was a pest she wanted to get rid of. 'If you no go, I call police. Maybe it make problem for your visa if police come.'

Hans didn't know what to do with himself. He didn't want to leave because it would feel like he was handing over the apartment and all the furniture to Dang. This is when he took out his phone and gave me a call. Simon to the rescue. Hans explained the situation to me very quickly. It was a Sunday morning and I was sitting in front of the TV with a cup of coffee when I got the call. I wasn't expecting to hear about a row over a condo and an affair with a ladyboy. The only advice I could give him was not to wait for the police to arrive.

'They will side with Thai people every time, not the farang,' I said. 'Pack up your stuff, go to a nearby hotel and go see a lawyer tomorrow.'

Hans followed my advice. He packed his bags and checked in to a cheap hotel nearby. As soon as he was settled into his new room, he gave Jasmine a call. They had another passionate night of sex and Hans was starting to see the silver lining in this unfortunate situation. He had lost a lovely partner in Dang, and he was on the verge of losing a lot of money, but he had found a gem in Jasmine. And, of course, he was now a functional lover for the first time in his life.

The next day Hans went to a lawyer in the town. He showed the lawyer the document that Dang had given him to show that he had paid one million baht towards the apartment. The lawyer told him in no uncertain terms that the document was not legally binding. He also explained that since Hans had paid for all the furniture in cash, there was no way to prove that he was the one who paid for it. Hans felt like such a fool. He cursed himself for being so naïve and paying for everything in cash. But he didn't dwell on these regrets for long. Hans had lost a lot of money and he felt cheated, but on the other hand he had found Jasmine. He looked forward to spending time with Jasmine and having a fulfilling sex life with a partner for the first time in his life. Hans rushed back to his new hotel room so that he could be with Jasmine, but when he arrived back at his hotel room, Jasmine was not there. He called her, but her phone was off. He called her dozens of times over the next few days, but she must have changed her number. Jasmine was gone. Hans never heard from her again.

Hans was alone again in Thailand, in an empty hotel room feeling lonely and foolish. He had plenty of time to reflect on his mistakes and think about how it had all gone wrong. Then one evening he had a bright idea. He logged into the dating website and filtered the search to 'ladyboys'.

A world of new opportunities opened up for Hans. He found a new way to enjoy his retirement in Thailand.

Hans visited me shortly after all this happened. When he told me about all the money he had lost, I felt devastated for him, but Hans was in surprisingly high spirits. He still had savings in his German back account and a decent monthly pension, and he was now free to travel around Thailand and enjoy himself. He was like a new man.

Mai's Tour Shop

When I managed a bar in Pattaya, one of the most interesting customers I met was an American guy named Joe. He was in his forties and he was an average-looking guy. He was about six foot tall, slim, and he had thinning brown hair. Joe walked into my bar one afternoon and we hit it off straight away. He started telling me about his job, and it was fascinating to listen to him. From a young age, Joe had been interested in boats and water. He started studying Oceanology – the seabed, the tides, the currents and so on. Joe entered USMMA (United States Merchant Marine Academy) where he studied for eight years. Oceanology was his passion. He gave his life to his studies and his work. When Joe left USMAA, he landed a job in a large cruise company. He started off as a ship's master and later became a ship's captain. My mouth hung open when Joe explained all this to me. I had never met anybody in this line of work before.

Joe never got married. He wanted to meet the right girl and settle down, but it just never happened for him. He probably didn't have many chances to meet women when he was out at sea, and when he was on shore he was busy studying. He was always studying something and aiming for some certificate that would qualify him to park various vessels in all the main harbours around the world. He seemed almost addicted to studying and getting all these different certifications.

Joe's company was based in America. He was out at sea for six weeks at a time, usually going down the east coast of America, around The Caribbean and down to South America. When he got back to shore, he had a four-week vacation before he was back out at sea again. Joe enjoyed his job, but his dream was to come live and work in Asia in a few years. He wanted to work for a cruise company that would require him to captain cruise ships from China, Korea and Japan, down to The Philippines, across to Singapore and through to the Indian Ocean. Captains earned great money on this route, but it would take Joe a couple of years of studying to get all the necessary certifications for the major harbours in Asia. So, over the next few years he planned to come to Asia for his vacations and study the coasts.

'Is that what brings you to Pattaya?' I joked with him. 'You came to study the coasts? You must be the only one.'

'No, no,' he laughed. 'This trip is purely pleasure. My father used to be in the army, and he always told me that there are certain places in Asia that I must visit, and amongst them were Bangkok, Pattaya and Phuket. I can't make it down to Phuket on this trip, but I plan to go there next year.'

Mai was born into a farming family in Isan. Her family was quite well-off compared to most farmers in Isan because they owned a lot of land and leased some of it to other farmers. Mai's parents wanted to give her a good education so that she wouldn't have to work the land when she grew up. So, they sent Mai to a private school in Bangkok when she was thirteen years old. Mai was a very hard-working student. She excelled at her new school and got into a good university. She was especially good at English, so Mai decided to major in Tourism. When she graduated, she got a job in the TAT (Tourism Authority of Thailand), which was based in Bangkok. When Mai was twenty-four, she had her first boyfriend. He was a Thai man and he treated Mai terribly. He mentally and physically abused her. The relationship lasted two years. Eventually Mai managed to get out of the relationship, but she was scarred by the experience. She decided to stay away from relationships in the future.

Despite two years of being stuck in a difficult relationship, Mai always did well at work, and after a few years she was promoted to a training position that brought her all around Thailand. Mai worked in this training position for a couple of years and as her twenty-eighth birthday approached she started to think a lot about her future. Her job was not as challenging or as rewarding as it once was, and she was sick of moving around Thailand to train employees of the TAT. In a few years she might be able to get another promotion and return to the head office in Bangkok, but that didn't really appeal to her either. After a few months of serious thought, Mai decided that she wanted to open her own tour shop. She had money saved and she knew the industry like the back of her hand. The only thing that she was not sure about was where to open her shop. This was back in 2003 / 2004 so several of the islands in the south of Thailand like Phuket and Koh Samui were already established tourist hot spots, but some islands like Kao Tao were developing and becoming more popular. It was a difficult decision, but eventually Mai chose to quit her job and set up her shop in Patong, Phuket. Mai chose Phuket because it had an international airport, it was connected to the mainland by a bridge, and there were dozens of islands nearby for tourists to enjoy on day tours. Mai knew that Patong was already saturated with travel shops, but she had a lot of experience in the tourism industry, so she fancied her chances.

About a year after I first met him, Joe finally visited Phuket on a two-week vacation, and he loved it. Joe had no interest in the bargirls and freelancers on Bangla Road, but he enjoyed the quieter bars and nice restaurants along the beach road. He also enjoyed different beaches around Phuket and during his second week in Phuket he was looking forward to going on some day tours to some of the islands around Phuket. Joe loved Phuket so much that he started to consider buying a condo there. He would be moving to Asia in a few years, so Phuket seemed like a nice place to set up home.

One night Joe was having a few beers in a bar along the beach road in Patong. After a few beers, he fancied a change of scenery so he paid his bill and walked down the road, away from Bangla Road, in search of a new bar. He saw a side street up ahead that he hoped would have some cosy, quiet bars, and as he turned onto this side street he almost bumped into a woman. Joe stopped in his tracks suddenly and looked down at the Thai woman. She was wearing a pink baseball cap backwards and a white tank top, and she was covered in paint.

'I'm terribly sorry,' she said. 'I didn't see you there. Please excuse me.'

She stepped to the side and walked passed Joe briskly. Joe was blown away by this woman's impeccable English. Her pronunciation and intonation were just like a native speaker. Joe turned around to watch her walk away. She looked beautiful even in those shabby clothes covered in paint. When the beautiful woman was out of sight, Joe turned back onto the side street and found a nice, cosy bar in which to sit and enjoy a few more beers.

The next evening Joe went back to the cosy bar and sat at a table overlooking the side street. Opposite the bar a couple of men were hard at work bringing two desks into a small store and setting up two computers and a printer. A Thai woman was standing outside the door supervising them. Joe was curious so he called out to the woman: 'What kind of shop will it be?'

'Travel shop,' she replied. 'It open in two days. Please come.'

A few days later, Joe went back to the cosy bar for a few more beers. He saw that the travel shop had opened, and the woman he had spoken to was sitting behind one of the computers. Joe didn't think much of it, but then he turned his head to see who was behind the other computer and he was surprised to see that it was the paint woman – the beautiful Thai woman he had almost bumped into a few days earlier. I've gotta talk to her, he said to himself. Joe finished his beer and walked over to the travel shop.

As soon as Joe walked into the shop, the pretty woman smiled and said: 'Oh, it's you.'

Joe was delighted that she remembered him. She looked even more beautiful this time, with long black hair, a blue shirt and thick frame glasses.

'Nice to see you again,' Joe said. 'What's your name?'

'My name is Mai,' She said, reaching out her hand above the computer monitor for a handshake.

Joe shook her hand and sat down. He told Mai that he wanted to go on a day tour around some islands. Mai took some brochures from the shelves on the wall, and in perfect English she started talking him through the most popular day tours around Phuket. Joe was only half listening because he was so taken aback by her English and her beauty. In the end he took half a dozen brochures and told Mai that he would come back the next day to book some tours. On his way back to his hotel, he thought to himself: wow! I've got to get a date with this girl.

Joe went back to Mai's travel shop the following day (a Wednesday), but, to Joe's disappointment, Mai was not there. The other woman, who Joe later found out was named Nan, asked if she could help, but Joe said that he wanted to only deal with Mai. Nan smiled at him and nodded. She could see that Joe liked Mai.

'She will be back in a few minutes,' Nan said to him. 'You can sit and wait.'

Mai came back to the shop about ten minutes later. Joe stood up to greet her as she entered. 'Oh, you are back,' Mai said, seemingly pleased to see Joe again.

Joe booked a popular island-hopping tour for Thursday, and he had no intention of leaving the shop without asking her out.

'Mai, you have been so helpful,' Joe started, a little nervously, 'so I was wondering if I could take you out to dinner this evening?'

Out of the corner of his eye, Joe could see Nan giggling.

'I'm sorry, I can't,' she said, almost automatically. 'I only opened this shop a few days ago, so I'm too busy these days.'

This was a big slap in the face for Joe. He felt embarrassed.

'No problem,' Joe said, and off he went with his tail between his legs.

Back in his hotel room, Joe was disheartened. When he asked Mai out for dinner, she didn't seem in the least bit interested in him. It had been years since Joe had felt this way about a girl, but Mai didn't seem to feel the same way about him. But Joe knew that time was on his side. He was due to leave Phuket in a few days, but he would be back again in a few months, and in a few years he would be based in Phuket, so he had plenty of reasons not to give up on Mai.

Joe had a great time on the island-hopping tour. He visited Maya Beach, Phi Phi Island, the James Bond Island in Phang Nga Bay, and a random island inhabited by monkeys. Joe found it a bit weird to see dozens of monkeys gathering on a beach and trying to get food from tourists, but apart from that Joe had an amazing time going around all the islands. The next morning Joe went to Mai's shop to tell her about the day tour, but, again, she was not there. Nan was there again, and there was also a boyish looking Thai girl called Far, who worked in the store part-time.

'When will Mai be back?' Joe asked Nan.

'In a few hours,' Nan said, giggling. 'You miss her?'

'Maybe,' Joe said, blushing. 'I want to bring her for dinner tonight to say thank you. Possible?'

'Today Mai birthday,' Nan said. 'We close shop 6 pm and go have small party on beach. You want come?'

Joe couldn't believe his ears. This was perfect!

'Yes, I'd love to come,' he said, barely able to conceal his excitement. 'What should I bring?'

'We bring food, you bring wine,' Nan said.

Joe was delighted. Faith had presented him with this glorious chance to spend time with Mai outside of the shop, and in the romantic setting of a picnic on the beach no less.

Right after he left the tour shop, he jumped in a taxi and headed to the nearest shopping mall. He bought two bottles of red and two bottles of white wine because he didn't know which one the girls preferred. He walked around the mall casually and thought about whether he should buy Mai a birthday present or not. He decided it would be nice to buy her something small, nothing too personal or expensive because they had only just met. Joe found a purple orchid in a beautifully decorated pot. He thought it would make the perfect gift for Mai because she could put it on her desk at work. It was simple and inexpensive, but it was a nice gesture.

Joe put on his nicest shorts and shirt, and he arrived at the beach thirty minutes early. While he was waiting, a freelancer sat next to him and kept asking if he wanted to go with her.

Please go away, he thought to himself, but he was too much of a gentleman to say this to her.

This freelancer was very persistent; she wouldn't take no for an answer.

'We can go drink beer together if you no want boom boom yet,' she said.

It was now 5:45. Joe didn't want Mai to see him talking to this woman. What would she think? He was starting to panic.

'My friends will come soon,' Joe said to her.

'No problem,' she said, nonchalantly.

Oh my God! Joe thought, take a hike, please.

'I want to be alone. Please leave,' Joe pleaded desperately.

'I just sit here and look at ocean same you,' she said, stubbornly.

It was now 5:50. Joe kept looking around to see if Mai and the girls were coming.

Joe moved twenty meters down the beach to get away from the freelancer, but she followed him.

'Where you from?' she asked Joe.

Joe sighed loudly and said 'I don't want to talk. Please go before my friends come.'

To Joe's despair, the freelancer didn't look like she was going anywhere. He considered walking to Mai's shop to meet the girls there or perhaps paying the freelancer to leave him alone. Fortunately for Joe, a few minutes before 6 o' clock, the freelancer spotted a drunken farang walking along the beach and she was off like a hunter to catch her prey. Joe breathed a sigh of relief.

Shortly after 6 pm, Joe saw Mai, Nan and Far walk towards him. They were busy chatting so they didn't see him at first, but Mai eventually looked up and saw Joe standing there. She was surprised. Mai looked at Nan for an explanation.

'I invited him,' Nan said. 'It's your birthday. More people, more fun.'

Joe didn't want Mai to feel uncomfortable by his presence, so he asked her: 'Is it okay?'

'Yes, of course,' Mai said, very brightly. 'I am glad to see you.

How was the day tour yesterday?'

Joe told Mai about the tour as they put down a mat on the beach and opened all the food. Nan handed Joe four plastic cups to pour the wine. They all ate plenty and drank plenty, and when the mood was at its highest they sang happy birthday for Mai. After a few hours, Nan and Far said they had to go somewhere. As Nan was standing up to go, she winked at Joe. He knew that Nan and Far were leaving so that he could have some time alone with Mai. Far had set up this whole situation for Joe, and he was very grateful to her.

Now that he was alone with Mai, Joe thought it was a good time to give her the birthday present he had prepared. Mai was very touched by Joe's gift.

'You can put it on your desk at work,' Joe said.

'Yes. I never got flowers before,' Mai said, placing her nose on the soft purple petals to take in the sweet scent. 'Thank you so much.'

Mai started asking Joe some questions about his job and about what he was doing in Phuket. Joe took a few minutes to explain about his job and his future plans to work in Asia and set up base in Phuket. Joe suddenly turned the tables on Mai and asked if she was ever married or had any kids.

Mai was a very private person, but perhaps because of the wine, she suddenly let her guard down and opened up to Joe. For the next twenty minutes Mai explained to Joe about how her ex-boyfriend treated her terribly for two years, and about how it put her off ever having another relationship with a man. Tears came to Mai's eyes as she spilled her heart out to Joe.

'That's why I focus so much on my work,' she concluded, sadly.

'I understand,' Joe said, sympathetically. 'I guess I use my job as a kind of escape too.'

They both sat in silence for a few minutes as Mai tried to stop crying.

'I'm sorry about this,' she said. 'I only met you a few days ago and here I am crying in front of you.'

'No, don't be sorry,' Joe said. 'I am so glad that you opened up to me.'

The party came to an end soon after Mai wiped her tears away.

Joe and May folded up the picnic mat and cleared away their trash. Joe walked Mia back to her shop. She was a little drunk, but she still wanted to open up for a few hours. On his way back to his hotel, Joe reflected on the evening. It had gone perfectly. He got to know Mai much better and he felt they had bonded during their short time together on the beach.

The next day Joe and Mai had lunch together. Joe was due to fly back to America late that night. He told Mai that he would be back in Phuket in six weeks and he hoped they could meet again and spend some time together.

'That would be nice,' Mai said, and she seemed genuinely interested in spending more time with Joe.

Joe and Mai felt very comfortable in each others' company. They made each other laugh and Mai's excellent English allowed them to speak freely about almost anything.

After lunch, Joe walked Mai back to her shop. It was especially hard for Joe to say goodbye to Mai this time because they were just starting to get to know each other. Joe was quickly falling in love with Mai, and he knew the next six weeks at sea would pass slowly without her.

Towards the end of November, a couple of weeks before Joe was due back in Phuket, Nan decided to give Joe and Mai's relationship another nudge in the right direction. One day they were talking together in the tour shop and Nan told Mai that there is more to life than work.

'I know you had a bad relationship before,' Nan said to her, 'but maybe it is time you try dating again. Joe will be back in a few weeks. I think he would be a good match for you. He is kind and gentle.'

'That's ridiculous,' Mai said, moving swiftly on to the next topic, but in truth Mai had already been thinking a lot about Joe.

Mai knew that he was boyfriend material, and if only she could open up and put her traumatic past behind her, she knew that she could have a meaningful relationship with Joe.

The Asian cruise company was eager to hire Joe. They said he could join their company in mid-February. On the first of December, Joe handed in his notice to the American company. He had two weeks' vacation and then he had to go back to America for his final six weeks at sea. On the third of December, Joe arrived in Phuket for a two-week visit. The sole purpose of this visit was to spend time with Mai. As soon as he checked in to his hotel, he rushed to her shop. Both Mai and Nan gave Joe a very warm welcome. Joe felt like he had returned home.

Joe told Mai that he wanted to take her for lunch.

May said, 'I'm busiest in the afternoon, but usually I have a couple of hours free from 5 to 7 pm. Would dinner be okay?'

'Yes. Can we have dinner every day while I'm here?' he asked, cheekily.

'Sure. Why not?' Mai said.

Joe was delighted because he now had a date with Mai set up for everyday of his two-week trip.

That evening over dinner, Mai was full of chat – much more than usual. Joe sensed that something had changed within Mai, so he bit the bullet and said, 'Mai, I remember during your birthday party at the beach you told me that you didn't want to get into another relationship with a man. But I really like you and I think we have something special. What do you think?'

Mai took a moment to consider her response.

'Actually, Nan spoke to me recently about this,' Mai said.

'Really? What did she say?'

'She said I should try dating again,' Mai said, and then she looked down at her food and added, 'with you.'

'Nan is very smart,' Joe said, giggling a little, 'So, can we start seeing each other?'

Mai nodded her head slowly a few times and then said shyly, 'Yes, I would like that.'

Joe reached across the table and held Mai's hand lovingly. They held hands for the rest of the meal. Just like that, they had become boyfriend and girlfriend.

Joe and Mai had dinner together every evening, and every morning Joe visited Mai's shop. He always brought coffee or some delicious bread or some Thai food. If there weren't any customers, he sat in the shop and chatted with Mai and Nan, and sometimes Far was there too. Joe and Mai got closer and closer as the days passed and their feelings for each other grew quickly. They held hands on the street and they hugged when they met and when they parted, but for the first week that was all the physical contact between them. One evening during the second week of Joe's visit, Joe and Mai enjoyed their first kiss on the beach. They shared a kiss every evening from then on, but it didn't go any further than that. They were both happy to take things slowly. On his last day in Phuket, Joe outlined his plans to Mai to assure her that they had a future together. Joe assured her that he wanted to buy a condo in Phuket and base himself there. He wanted to start a new life in Phuket, and he was so happy that Mai would be a part of it.

It was turning out to be the perfect love story – the allusive happy Thai love story. It looked like nothing could go wrong, but then disaster struck. On the morning of December 26th 2004, the biggest tsunami in Asian history struck, claiming almost quarter of a million lives in fourteen countries across Asia, including over five thousand confirmed deaths in Thailand. A thirty-meter wave hit Patong beach in Phuket, flooding the area and causing destruction on a huge scale. Many of the buildings in this area were poorly and cheaply constructed, so they were flattened by the tsunami. There was no warning system in the Indian Ocean, so the tsunami came as a complete surprise to the tourists and the Thai people in Patong.

Joe was out at sea around The Caribbean at the time. As soon as he heard the news, he called Mai's shop, but the line was dead. Horrible thoughts started running through his head. He felt sick with worry. He imagined the tsunami hitting Patong and carrying Mai away. Joe's head was spinning with these horrible images. He called Mai's shop again, but of course it was still dead. Joe suddenly realized that the landline of Mai's shop was the only way he had of contacting her. He didn't have her mobile phone number or email, nor did he have Nan or Far's phone numbers. And to make it even worse, Mai didn't have Joe's contact information.

This was an absolutely horrific time for Joe and anybody else who had loved ones in Patong and other areas hit by the tsunami; the not-knowing was torture. He didn't know if she was alive and well, or if she had been taken from him, or if she had been seriously injured. All he could do was wait.

Joe could not go back to Phuket until the end of January. It was the longest month of Joe's life. For that month, Joe used his free time looking carefully through all the footage and images he could find of Phuket in the aftermath of the tsunami. He desperately hoped that he would see Mai in one of the pictures or videos. He spent countless hours searching, but it was all in vain. In late January, he flew into Phuket airport. All the hotels that were opened around Patong and the other tourist areas were full with construction workers and people who had lost their homes in the tsunami. The only hotel that Joe could find with an available room was near the airport, about thirty minutes from Patong. Joe got a taxi to the hotel and told the driver to wait while he checked in and dropped off his bags. Joe was back in the taxi within ten minutes and off he went to Patong. The main road into Patong brings you up a hill first and gives you a view of Patong from up high. When the taxi reached the top of the hill, the landscape in front of them suddenly changed. A devastated Patong stretched out below them —destruction everywhere. As the taxi entered Patong, Joe looked out his window at the damaged buildings and the endless piles of rubble at the side of the road. It was hard for the taxi driver to manoeuvre his way through some parts of Patong because there was so much construction going on. As the taxi got nearer to the beach, Joe's heart was in his mouth because he was getting closer and closer to Mai's shop.

Joe got out of the taxi before it reached the beachfront road. He wanted to walk the last couple of hundred meters to Mai's shop and use this time to prepare himself for what he might find. As soon as he turned on to the side street off the beach road, he saw that Mai's shop and the other shops on that side had been completely destroyed, and all that remained was rubble. Among this rubble Joe could see pieces of Mai's desk. Everything else was unrecognizable. On the other side of the street, the cosy bar that Joe used to visit was still standing, but the roof had been ripped off and the inside of the bar had been gutted. It was now just a shell of a store with a back wall, a side wall and a bare concrete floor. Joe stood outside Mai's shop for a while in the hope that she might suddenly turn up. He asked passers-by if they knew what had happened to the owner of the tour shop, but nobody knew anything. He found a picture of Mai on his phone and showed people, but nobody recognized her. Then he started walking up along Bangla Road, the second street in from the beach and all the little side streets in between. He didn't recognize anybody. There were some pop-up stores and restaurants open, so Joe asked the workers about Mai, but nobody could help him. Joe had waited for over a month for the chance to come to Phuket and search for

Mai, but now that he was on the scene, he realized he had no way of finding her. He didn't even know Mai's full name or where she lived.

Joe started walking along the beach and he saw two policemen up ahead. He approached them and explained that he was looking for his girlfriend. The policemen informed Joe that a tsunami information centre had been set up alongside the beach near Bangla Road. Joe hurried to the centre and he was delighted to find a woman who spoke good English. Joe explained the situation, but when the woman asked for the full Thai names of the people he was looking for, all Joe could give her was 'Mai, Nan and Far.'

'Those names could be anybody,' she said. 'I only have a record of the Thai names of the people who passed away or who are missing. I can't help you unless you have their full Thai names.'

Joe looked lost. He didn't know where to turn next. The woman told Joe that he could go to the morgue and look through the pictures of the people who had passed away, but Joe could not face that. He couldn't bring himself to look through hundreds of pictures of dead bodies. It just wasn't an option for him. Instead, he walked the streets of Patong for the next five days with Mai's picture in his phone, asking hundreds of people if they had seen her. From early in the morning until night, he pounded the pavements of Patong, but he didn't find a single lead to Mai's whereabouts. It was a lost cause. He now had only a couple of days left before he had to start his new job in the Asian company. Joe decided to fly to Bangkok for his last few days. He planned to come back to Phuket again in a few months and renew his search for Mai.

During his first day in Bangkok, Joe was walking along Sukhumvit Road and he spotted a bar that he liked between Soi 4 and Soi 5. He ordered a beer and slumped down in his chair. He was having a horrible time of it. He had lost his potential future wife in the cruellest of ways and he was slowly coming to the realization that he might never find out what happened to her. And to think that he had to start a new job in a few days in this frame of mind.

'Joe.' He heard his name being called.

Joe turned around to see who was calling him. No, it wasn't Mai. It was me.

It had been about a year since Joe had walked into my bar in Pattaya, but I always remembered him because he was such a fascinating guy. Fortunately, Joe recognized me too. Joe gave me a big hug. He must have been happy to see a familiar face. Joe spent the next thirty minutes spilling his heart out to me about Mai. I was devastated for him when I heard what had happened. From the way Joe was talking, I could tell that he didn't hold out much hope of ever finding Mai.

'I still have contact with some of the girls from my old bar,' I told Joe, desperate to help in any way I could. 'They might have contact with some girls in Phuket. I'll ask around.'

'That would be great,' Joe said, but he knew it was a long shot.

Joe showed me a picture of Mai on his phone, and he transferred it to my computer so that I could show it to people. We chatted for a couple of hours over a few beers and at the end of the evening we exchanged emails. I told him I would contact him if I found anything. He flew to Singapore the next day to start his new job.

This was early 2005. I had left the bar scene in Pattaya and I was due to get married a few weeks later in Bangkok. The day after I met Joe, I reached out to the mamasan who used to work in my old bar, but she didn't have any contacts in Patong. I also contacted several of the girls from my old bar, but they weren't much help either. Then a few days before my wedding, Andy, a friend of mine from the UK, contacted me out of the blue. He had just arrived in Phuket, where he owned a condo, and he said he hoped to come up to Bangkok for my wedding. I sent Andy a picture of Mai and asked him to show it around and ask about her. Andy said he knew a lot of people in Patong so he would be happy to help.

My wife and I had a lovely ceremony in Bangkok. It was well attended by our family and good friends, including Andy. We all had food and drinks together in the evening. It was a great day. Andy and I were staying in the same hotel, so the next morning we found ourselves chatting over a coffee. We were chatting about how well the wedding had gone, when Andy suddenly said 'Oh, by the way, I found that girl.'

'What girl?'

'Mai.'

I was shocked. 'Mai from the tour shop?' I asked.

'Yes, that girl.'

I was so taken aback by this that I started muttering like a fool: 'What? Where? Are you sure it's her?'

'It's her alright,' he said. 'They are building a shopping complex behind second road in Patong, and behind that there is a row of new stores, and one of them is a tour shop. It had an email café next store. I popped into the tour shop to ask if they had seen the girl in the photo. But before I even asked, I noticed that one of the girls at the computers was the girl in the photo. I took a picture of her. Look.'

Andy showed me the picture on his phone, and, sure enough, it was Mai. There were two girls next to her, who I assumed were Nan and Far, but I couldn't be sure because I had never seen them before.

'And I got this too,' Andy said, handing me a brochure from the shop.

At the bottom of the brochure Mai had written the name of her shop 'Mai's Tour Shop' and her phone number.

Andy found her. I couldn't believe it!

My wife and I were due to get a bus to her village that morning. I got the brochure and photo from Andy, and on my way to my wife's village, I thought about how I should give Joe the news. I decided that words were not necessary, and the best way would be to just send him the picture of Mai and her new phone number. When I arrived at my wife's village, I connected my laptop to the internet and emailed Joe the photo and phone number. Within a few minutes he sent me an email, asking me where I found her, how I found her, and so on.

'Just call her,' I replied.

The next day Joe sent me an update. He called Mai and they chatted about everything that had happened. Fortunately, Mai, Nan and Far had not been hurt in the tsunami. By a remarkable stroke of fortune, on the morning of the tsunami, they all went to a restaurant up in the hills to have breakfast with a group of Malaysian customers. Joe didn't explain all the details to me, but he thanked me and Andy for all our help.

In September that year, my wife and I held a Thai wedding ceremony in her village, and then we flew down to Phuket for our honeymoon. We arranged to meet Joe on the beach road, and of course he came to meet us with Mai by his side. Over dinner, Joe told me that he bought a condo in Patong, the new job was going well, and he and Mai were planning to get married. We talked for hours. It was lovely to see Joe and Mai together. They were a lovely couple. At the end of the evening, Joe said he had a wedding present for me and my wife. He handed us an envelope with a large amount of money inside. I wasn't expecting anything. Seeing Joe and Mai reunited was reward enough for me, but it was a lovely gesture all the same.

So, there you have it: The allusive happy Thai love story. Just like in any other country, it is possible if you find the right person.

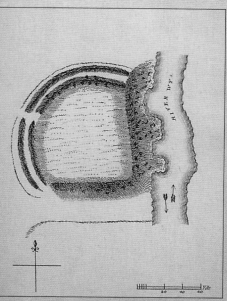

Chepstou... near the ... south Wa... can be se... There are ... Monmou... north of ... 162 (NGR ST533941).

Main Picture: *A distant view of Chepstow Castle and town, painted by Cornelius Pearson, 1844 (By permission of the National Library of Wales).*

...epstow Bulwarks Camp is situated near the town's suburb ...Bulwark. It is located at the end of Alpha Road. This plan ...the hillfort comes from William Coxe's An Historical Tour ...Monmouthshire (London 1810). OS 1:50,000 sheet 162 ...GR ST538927).

Runston Church is situated near Crick, a short distance off the A48, some 3 miles (4.8km) south-west of Chepstow. It is situated on farm land, and visitors should take care to close gates and keep to the path. OS 1:50,000 sheet 162 (NGR ST495916).

Chepstow Castle: A Structural History

Introduction

The arms of the Marshal family, earls of Pembroke. The same arms were later born by Roger Bigod III earl of Norfolk. The Marshals held the lordship of Chepstow through the first half of the thirteenth century and were eventually succeeded by Bigod in 1270. Together, they were among the most formidable builders of the magnificent castle.

C HEPSTOW CASTLE IS ONE OF THE KEYS OF WALES, guarding the river crossing near the mouth of the Wye where the main coastal land route from southern England enters Wales. Above Chepstow are the river cliffs of the Wye Valley, with no usable crossing until Monmouth is reached. Ships from Bristol, Gloucester or further afield could bring supplies to the castle, and the timber and iron industries of the Wye Valley and Dean Forest — like the castle — already existed by the time of Domesday Book. From medieval times until the last century, Chepstow was a flourishing small port, as the many pleasant pre-nineteenth-century houses in the town remind us.

Chepstow is perched high on a river cliff overlooking the Wye, and guards one of the main crossing points from England into Wales. Here, the east end of the castle straddles a great cleft in the cliff face through which supplies could be hoisted into the cellars from a boat anchored below.

Sketch Map of South-East Wales showing the Lordship of Chepstow *(Strigoil)*

(After William Rees)

From about 1119 until 1245, Caerleon, Usk and Trellech were held in common with Chepstow by a branch of the de Clare family and then by the Marshals. Thereafter their descent was divided and they were held by different Marcher families.

Abergavenny

Monmouth

TRELLECH

Trellech

River Wye

USK

Usk

River Usk

Tintern Abbey ✝

(STRIGOIL)

CHEPSTOW

■ **Chepstow**

Caerleon

CALDICOT

Caerwent

Caldicot

CAERLEON

Mouth of the Severn

N

Miles   0   5

Km   0   8

One of the carved figures which adorn the battlements of Marten's Tower. These figures were perhaps added about 1310.

Few castles in these islands tell the story of medieval castle-building, from beginning to [en]d, as does Chepstow. It was built in four [su]ccessive stages, with later domestic [alt]erations in Tudor times and a remodelling [of] the defences for cannon and musketeers [aft]er the Civil War. William fitz Osbern's stone [ke]ep *(Chepstow 1)*, built within a decade of [10]66, still forms its core. Its vulnerable east [sid]e was strengthend by William Marshal, earl [of] Pembroke, in about 1200 with a curtain [wa]ll and two flanking towers equipped with [arr]owslits, in the new defensive mode of the [thi]rteenth century. As such it is one of the [ear]liest examples of this new style of [for]tification in the country *(Chepstow 2)*. [W]illiam Marshal's sons greatly enlarged the [ca]stle, adding the gatehouse, through which [th]e visitor now enters, and the ward behind it. [Th]ey also heightened fitz Osbern's keep and [bui]lt a strongly-defended barbican at the [up]per end of the castle. This work forms [Ch]epstow 3. Anselm Marshal, last of his line, [die]d in 1245. Chepstow later passed to his [sis]ter's grandson, Roger Bigod III, earl of [No]rfolk, a rich magnate at the court of [Ed]ward I. Between 1270 and 1300 Bigod

equipped the castle with accommodation appropriate to his rank and to the size of his considerable household, including a large hall block in the lower ward (on the right as the visitor enters the castle) and a tower opposite with a private suite of rooms for his own use *(Chepstow 4)*. Ironically this tower does not now bear his name, but that of Henry Marten, one of the men who signed the death warrant of King Charles I, and who was imprisoned in it for many years after the Restoration of Charles II. Roger Bigod also built the town wall and gate, which still encircle Chepstow. There were no major additions to the castle after his death.

3

Chepstow 1: William fitz Osbern — The First Norman Castle (1067-1075)

'Castellum de Estrighoiel fecit Wilhelmus Comes'

'EARL WILLIAM BUILT THE CASTLE of Estriguil'. So Domesday Book of 1086 records that the founder of Chepstow Castle was William fitz Osbern, lord of the small Norman town of Breteuil in Calvados, and a close political colleague and companion in arms of William the Conqueror. The Conqueror created him earl of Hereford a few months after the battle of Hastings and William built the first castle at Chepstow as a base for his conquest of the Welsh kingdom of Gwent. Outside the gates of his castle a small town of English and Norman settlers grew up, in which fitz Osbern founded a Benedictine priory — now the parish church — as a cell of the monastery he founded at Cormeilles, north of Lisieux in Normandy. The town was known as *Cheap-stow* — 'the market town'. In time, this English name came to replace the Welsh *Ystraigyl* — 'the bend of the river' — (sometimes anglicized as Strigoil) as the name of the castle.

William fitz Osbern died in battle at Casse in Flanders in 1071. Four years later his son, Roger of Breteuil, rebelled against the king and forfeited his lands. The castle must have been completed by then, if not by the time of his father's death.

It was sited on a long, narrow ridge of carboniferous limestone running east — wes parallel to the river. The Wye had cut into th northern flank of this ridge forming high an impregnable river cliffs which made artificial defences unnecessary on this side. To the south, the ridge was flanked by a narrow steep-sided valley, so that here the castle sat on top of a substantial natural rock slope, which itself formed a defence against the siege methods of the day. On the highest an narrowest point of the ridge stands fitz Osbern's rectangular hall-keep, relying on th passive defensive strength of its masonry fo protection. This can best be seen from outsi the castle on the south, where the cliff-like, buttressed face of the keep, without window or arrowloops, contrasts with buildings of later periods with their projecting circular towers equipped with batteries of arrowslits covering the ground in front of the walls with a deadly cross fire. O each side of the keep, a stone walled bailey along the line of the ridge, containing the wooden buildings of the garrison, with thei stables, granaries, chapel and the like.

Earl William's hall-keep is the earliest datable secular stone building in Britain. T

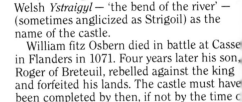

Left: A scene from the magnificent Bayeux Tapestry depicting a heavily-armoured Norman horseman at the battle of Hastings. A S foot soldier lies mortally wounded. William fitz Osbern, builder of Chepstow, offered 60 of his own ships as a contribution to William Conquerer's invasion fleet, and commanded the right wing of the a at Hastings.

Below: *The opening of the Gloucestershire section of the Domesda Book, records that* 'Earl William built the castle of Chepstow' *(he 'Estrighoiel'). Within months of the Norman invasion, fitz Osbern's loyalty to the Conqueror had been rewarded with the earldom of Hereford. Shortly afterwards, he began the construction of Chepsto Castle (Copyright: Public Record Office, E31/2, f. 162a).*

...tist's impression of Chepstow 1 — William fitz Osbern's castle as it ...have appeared about 1067-75 (Illustration by John Banbury).

The twelfth-century rectangular keep at Falaise in Normandy, birthplace of William the Conqueror. The Chepstow hall-keep is very like such contemporary Norman work. The round keep to the rear is later and dates from the time of King Philip Augustus (1180-1223), whose work in France was in turn to influence William Marshal's (pp. 6-7) building at Chepstow (Photograph by Peter Humphries).

...d seated in hall amid his followers was a ...werful medieval symbol of lordship. The ...liest halls had been barn-like buildings of ...ber, but by about A.D. 1000 rectangular ...ne halls were being built in several parts of ...stern Europe, both as signs of lordly ...stige and for defence and

Benedictine priory at ...stow, now St Mary's ...sh church. Founded ... after the castle, it ...a daughter house of ...monastery established ...illiam fitz Osbern at ...neilles in Normandy ...055.

protection in the unsettled time when the empire of Charlemagne had broken up into warring localized lordships. This was the birth of the stone castle of the Middle Ages and the hall-keep at Chepstow is very like some of the early defensive halls built about this time in western France. It is not yet a tower, as later Norman keeps were to be, but a fortified rectangular stone hall of two storeys.

About 1115 Henry I granted Chepstow to the de Clare family, and it remained with them for most of the century. The castle was stronger than most others of its day and needed no new fortification. Earl Richard de Clare — known as Strongbow — conqueror of Irish Leinster, died in 1176, leaving a daughter Isabella as heiress to vast estates in Normandy, England and Wales and Ireland. For thirteen years, until her marriage, Chepstow was in the hands of the king.

Chepstow 2: William Marshal the Elder — New Methods of Defence (*c.* 1200)

WILLIAM MARSHAL WAS ONE of the outstanding men of his day, a landless son of an English, knightly family, who had made a name for himself in Angevin France by his formidable fighting ability and by his uncompromising loyalty to those he served.

This handsome tomb effigy in the Temple Church, City of London is believed to be that of the dashing William Marshal the elder, earl of Pembroke (d. 1219), marshal of England and builder of the second major phase at Chepstow.

He stayed loyal to the old king, Henry II, when almost all others deserted him for his rebel sons. Richard 'Lionheart', one of these sons, respected Marshal both for his loyalty his father and for his skill as a soldier (he ha unhorsed Richard in a skirmish, but spared his life). When Richard became king he married William to *la pucelle d'Estriguil* — '*T Maid of Chepstow'*, the heiress Isabella de Clare. The phrase comes from a spirited vers biography in medieval French, which makes William Marshal one of the few men of his a who appears to us, to some extent, as an individual rather than as an anonymous figure in a suit of mail or a bishop's mitre.

William fitz Osbern's castle had now stood unchanged for nearly a century and a half. William Marshal, however, was a notable castle builder who remodelled several strongholds in the up to date techniques of military architecture familiar to him from his career in France. His most impressive work i the great round keep at Pembroke, guarding the sea route between his British and Irish lands. Marshal also built the castle at Usk,

The great round keep dominates the inner ward at Pembroke Castle. Built around 1190-1200, it is perhaps William Marshal's most impressive work.

north-west of Chepstow. At Chepstow itself, he rebuilt the east curtain wall of the castle, with two round towers projecting out from the wallface, to protect this vulnerable side where approach was possible along level ground. The circular shape of his towers gav an all-round field of fire, so that the ground i

nt of the castle could be covered by cross-
 from the arrowslits in the towers and
lls. A generation later — as we can see at
epstow — the entrance to so important a
tle would have been guarded by a
ehouse with a strongly-defended entrance
ssage between two round towers, but such
ehouses, though used by the Romans,
re not yet in use for castles. The entrance
William Marshal's castle is a simple pointed
h through the curtain, without a portcullis
d protected only by its siting between one
the two towers, which covers it at close
ge, and the river cliff.
The wall and towers were built of the grey-
ite Carboniferous limestone on which the

castle stands, but this did not lend itself to
being dressed into squared blocks for the
sides of doors and arrowslits, and for this
purpose a fine creamy-yellow Jurassic
limestone was brought by sea from the
quarries on Dundry Hill outside Bristol. The
high quality Dundry stone is characteristic of
Chepstow 2 and the earlier stages of
Chepstow 3.

*An artist's impression of Chepstow 2 — William Marshal's castle as it
may have appeared about 1200 (Illustration by John Banbury).*

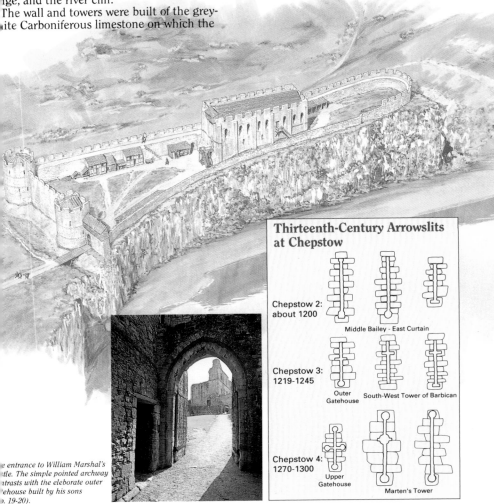

**Thirteenth-Century Arrowslits
at Chepstow**

Chepstow 2:
about 1200

Middle Bailey - East Curtain

Chepstow 3:
1219-1245

Outer
Gatehouse   South-West Tower of Barbican

Chepstow 4:
1270-1300   Upper
Gatehouse

Marten's Tower

*e entrance to William Marshal's
tle. The simple pointed archway
itrasts with the eleborate outer
ehouse built by his sons
. 19-20).*

Chepstow 3: The Younger Marshals — The Castle Englarged (1219-1245)

WILLIAM MARSHAL DIED at Whitsun 1219, leaving five sons, all of whom succeeded in turn to their father's inheritance and all of whom died childless by 1245, by which time the castle had been much enlarged and strengthened. William the eldest son, continued his father's building work at Chepstow and in March 1228 received a gift from the king of ten oaks from the Forest of Dean for 'work in the tower *(turris)* of Chepstow'. We cannot date the various phases of enlargement of the castle by the younger Marshals closely, but here 'the tower' is probably fitz Osbern's old hall-keep. The first floor of this was remodelled with large two-light windows in the safe riverward side and a second floor was added over its western third, its end wall supported on a large arch spanning the hall, the springing of which can still be seen (p. 41). All the architectural details are in a creamy-yellow Dundry limestone. This new upper storey probably contained a private chamber for the younger William Marshal and his wife.

The rectangular tower at the angle of th upper bailey is at least as early, and may ev have been begun by the elder William Marshal, together with the gateway and curtain wall beside it. The gateway is a sim pointed arch with no portcullis and there i free use of high quality squared masonry o Dundry stone. Inside the tower there was a gracefully proportioned room over a cellar. This may have been the *camera comitisse* — private room of the countess — mentioned a thirteenth-century document. If so, it wo be tempting to see it as accommodation fo the dowager countess, William Marshal the elder's widow, who as the *pucelle d'Estrigoi* had brought the vast de Clare estates to th family by marriage.

The first phase of Chepstow 3 thus provi two sets of domestic accommodation of hig quality grouped around the upper bailey, which itself may have been a court or garde giving some measure of privacy to their occupants. The gift of oaks may have been intended for roofing the new rooms in the tower and this phase of work may thus have been nearing completion as the new buildi season opened in the spring of 1228.

An artist's impression of Chepstow 3 — the Younger Marshals' castl it may have appeared about 1245 (Illustration by John Banbury).

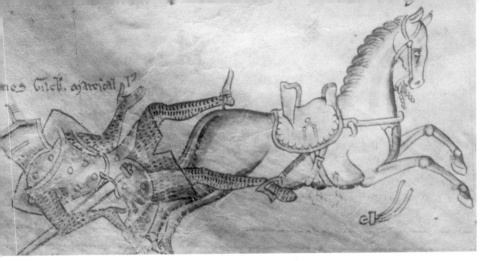

ᵣrt Marshal succeeded his brother, Richard, as earl of Pembroke in
and soon began a vigorous programme of building at Chepstow.
ᵣrt died in 1241, from injuries sustained during a fall in a
ᵤament at Ware, Hertfordshire. This manuscript illustration from
ᵤhew Paris's Chronica Majora — depicting Gilbert dragged by his
ₑ during the fall — dates from about 1250 (By kind permission of
ᵤasters and Fellows of Corpus Christi College, Cambridge, Ms. 16,
ᵤ8).

Villiam Marshal the younger died in 1231.
ₛ brother Richard quarrelled with the king
1 after what almost amounted to a minor
al civil war, he withdrew to Ireland, where

was killed in 1234. It is doubtful whether
ᵤch new work could have been put in hand
this unsettled time, but his brother Gilbert,
ₒ succeeded him, began a vigorous
ᵢlding programme. He received several gifts
ₒaks from the king in 1234, for work at the
ₛtle and for the repair of Chepstow bridge.
ₑ later work of Chepstow 3, after that on
ₑ keep and upper bailey, falls into two parts.
ₑ first consisted of the filling in of the ditch
ₙting the east curtain of Chepstow 2 and

the adding of the lower bailey, with its curtain
wall, great gatehouse, probably a now
vanished corner tower on the site of the later
Marten's Tower and the tower on the curtain
wall of the middle bailey. Here the Dundry
stone is still used for dressings, though
architectural details and the forms of arrowslit
used suggest that it is later than the work on
the upper bailey.

In the final phase of Chepstow 3, the
creamy-yellow Dundry stone is replaced by
purple-red sandstone of Devonian age,
quarried from local beds of 'Old Red'
sandstone, to replace the expensive imported
freestone. The distinction between them is
not always clear cut, partly because of later
repairs and patching and partly because a
small amount of Dundry stone may have been
kept in stock — or been available for reuse
from demolished structures — for work
requiring high-quality stone. The red
sandstone is particularly characteristic of the
barbican added at the upper end of the castle,
with its batteries of arrowloops protecting this
potentially vulnerable flank of the castle, and
of the arcaded gallery in the narrow passage
between the keep and the river cliff. The
gallery aided the defence of the castle by
helping to divide it into a series of water-tight
compartments which could each be held
separately in case of need. Though we cannot
date these various phases exactly, they would
probably have kept the Chepstow
stonemasons busy from the resumption of
work in 1234 until the death of Anselm
Marshal in 1245 marked the end of his line.

Chepstow 4: Roger Bigod III — A Nobleman's Residence (1270-1300)

ON THE DEATH OF THE LAST of the Marshal brothers, their lands were divided amongst their sisters, Chepstow passing to the eldest, Maud, and on her death to her son, Roger Bigod II, earl of Norfolk. On his death in 1270 his son, another Roger Bigod, inherited. Whereas his father was mainly interested in his East Anglian lands, Roger Bigod III took an active interest in his Marcher lordship. He was a generous patron of Tintern Abbey, and was regarded as its 'second founder'. He enclosed Chepstow with a town wall which in large part still survives. Earl Roger also equipped the castle with accommodation worthy of a nobleman of high rank and his numerous household.

Some of Roger Bigod's financial accounts have survived and these enable us to follow the progress of his works at Chepstow, at least in broad outline. Despite the addition of the barbican, the security of the western flank of the castle evidently still gave cause for concern, for the first work — undertaken about 1272 — was the strengthening of the upper gatehouse in the barbican with a gate tower and portcullis. The next six years (1272-78) may have seen the building of the town wall. Although this period also saw the beginning of the final conquest of independent Wales by King Edward I, several serious Welsh revolts ensued, and it would have been prudent to protect the town in this way whilst matters were still unsettled.

Work at the castle began again about 1278, under the direction of Master Ralf, who was paid a wage of two shillings a week as master mason. Between about 1278 and 1285 a fine new hall range was built against the river cliff, along the northern side of the lower bailey (pp. 21-31). This was followed in about 1285-93 by Marten's Tower at the south-east corner of the same bailey, a vulnerable angle of the defences. The tower also provided private accommodation — and if necessary a military command post — for Earl Roger.

Finally, in about 1293-1300 the great tower (William fitz Osbern's keep) was enlarged and the upper storey, added to its western third by

the younger Marshals, was extended along the full length of the building. In 1298-99 a military engineer named Reginald was brought in to advise on the building of four large 'springalds' or catapults mounted on four of the towers, including the great tower. For some reason these were later neglected and three of them were put into store, where they soon became useless. Roger Bigod's building work was not confined to the castle and town walls of Chepstow, and he largely paid for the splendid new abbey church for the Cistercian monks at Tintern. Its high altar and eastern parts were ready for use in 1288 and, when it was finished, Bigod's arms commemorated his generosity in the stained glass of the east window.

Artist's impression of Chepstow 4 — Roger Bigod III's castle as it ...have appeared around 1300 (Illustration by John Banbury).

...seal of Roger Bigod III, earl of Norfolk (d. 1306) under whose ...tion the fourth phase of major building work was undertaken at ...stow. As well as developing the defensive capabilities of the castle, ...d improved the domestic accommodation to a standard ...nensurate with his rank and status as a great nobleman and ...hal of England (Copyright: Public Record Office, E26/1 seal 78).

The east end of the abbey church at Tintern. Bigod's generous patronage to the monks at Tintern largely financed the thirteenth-century rebuilding of the church and was commemorated in the stained glass of the great east window.

Partly because of his lavish building works, Roger Bigod was heavily in debt in his later years. In 1302 the childless earl made an agreement with the king that in return for an annuity, his lands and castles would pass to the Crown on his death.

The Later Middle Ages

ROGER BIGOD III DIED in 1306 and his lands passed to the king. With Edward I's conquest of independent Wales, Chepstow's military role declined. Bigod, short of money, may have left parts of his planned work unfinished and shortly after his death parts of the castle were described as 'ruinous and unroofed'. Building work seems to have been in progress in 1308-10, when many oaks were cut in Wentwood 'for the repair and altering of the castle of Chepstow'. It is possible that the parapets of Marten's Tower with their sculptured figures may date from this time, for they are constructed in slightly different masonry from the rest of the tower, and other such sets of figures elsewhere are of similar date. King Edward II granted Chepstow to his half brother, Thomas de Brotherton, but for some years it was in the hands of the king's unscrupulous favourite, Hugh le Despenser the younger, who built up a substantial power base in south Wales. When he fell from power in 1326 he fled to Chepstow with his father and the king. They tried to escape by boat to

Ireland but the tides were against them and they were forced to land at Cardiff. All three were later captured. The Despensers were executed and the king was later murdered at Berkeley Castle in Gloucestershire.

The castle later passed to de Brotherton's descendant Thomas Mowbray, duke of Norfolk. In 1403 he was ordered to garrison against Owain Glyndŵr with 20 men at arms and 60 archers, but Owain's advance was halted at Usk, and Chepstow saw no action. During the Wars of the Roses, Chepstow was again the refuge of fallen royal favourites when Richard Woodville, earl Rivers and his son, Sir John Woodville, the rivals of Warwick 'the Kingmaker' fled here after their defeat at Edgecote in July 1469. Warwick pursued them. The Chepstow garrison handed the unpopular Woodvilles over to him without a fight and they were later beheaded. Chepstow had recently passed into the hands of their ally William Herbert, earl of Pembroke, who was also executed after Edgecote, but the Herberts soon recovered from this setback and came to dominate the area politically, with many of its castles.

Although beheaded after the battle of Edgecote in 1469, William Herbert left Chepstow to his widow who outlived him by fifteen years. The Herberts continued to hold the castle, together with many other south-east Wales, for the remainder of the fifteenth century. In this manuscript illustration, Sir William and his wife Anne are seen kneeling before King Edward IV (By permission of the British Library Ms. 18 D II, f.6).

In the early fourteenth century, Chepstow was held briefly by the unscrupulous favourite of King Edward II, Hugh le Despenser the younger. This depiction of Despenser comes from a stained glass window of about 1340-44 at Tewkesbury Abbey (By kind permission of the Vicar and Churchwardens at Tewkesbury Abbey).

Tudor Chepstow

N THE SIXTEENTH CENTURY the
Somersets, earls of Worcester, still
ontrolled much of the affairs of the new
ounty of Monmouth from their castle at
aglan. At Chepstow, many of the buildings
round the lower bailey were converted into
dgings for their numerous household. Most
these were half-timbered ranges built
gainst the earlier curtain walls, and have
ow vanished, but inserted windows, doors
d fireplaces show their presence. The more

*liam Somerset (1527?-89), third earl of Worcester, whose family
*trolled much of the affairs of the new county of Monmouth in the
*eenth century. The Somersets concentrated their building works on
ir major castle at Raglan. Nevertheless, new lodgings for their
usehold servants are witnessed at Chepstow by numerous inserted
orways, windows and fireplaces, particularly in the lower bailey (By
d permission of his grace the duke of Beaufort).*

aceable age permitted the opening of large
o- and three-light windows in the outside
lls of the great gatehouse, which was
modelled internally with new fireplaces,
rhaps in its traditional role of residence of
e steward. The rooms in Marten's Tower
re made lighter by the insertion of large
ctangular windows. The curtain wall
tween the middle and lower baileys had a
o storey range built against it on both sides,
rhaps in the time of King Henry VIII. This
s vanished, but the line of its roof can be
en against the face of the more northerly
ver, which was turned into a small kitchen.
o large rectangular fireplaces of this date
rvive in the face of the curtain wall, the
ad of the lower fireplace being of white
tton limestone from the quarries near
rthcawl in Glamorgan.

Chepstow Castle and the Civil War

AT THE OUTBREAK OF the Civil War,
Henry earl of Worcester, a Roman
Catholic, declared for King Charles I. For most
of the war Chepstow and the Forest of Dean
lay between Royalist Gwent and the strongly
Puritan city of Gloucester. Chepstow also
controlled a major cross-channel route
between south Wales, source of much of the
Royalist infantry, and Bristol, a key Royalist
base for operations in southern England
throughout most of the war. In April 1643, the
Parliamentary general William Waller

Above: *A letter written by Edward Herbert of Raglan to Captain Thomas
Morgan, the Royalist commander of Chepstow, instructing him in the
urgent movement of troops and artillery before Waller's attack on
Monmouthshire in 1643 (Gwent County Record Office, Misc. Mss, 1351;
published in J.E. Lee, Isca Silurum, London 1862).*
Below: *Edward Somerset (1601-67), Lord Herbert, whose wealthy
father the fifth earl of Worcester had declared for King Charles I, was
appointed commander of the Royalist troops in south Wales in 1642
(Photograph by the Courtauld Institute of Art, by kind permission of his
grace the duke of Beaufort).*

advanced into Gwent with a mobile column, but lacking heavy artillery he was unable to reduce Chepstow and the other Gwent castles and was forced to withdraw. There were other raids and skirmishes in and around Chepstow and the parish registers record the burials of a number of officers and men killed in the fighting, but it was not until October 1645, with the king's cause rapidly becoming hopeless, that Parliamentary artillery finally enforced the surrender of Chepstow's garrison of 64 men and 17 cannon.

In 1648, during the second Civil War, the castle was seized by a local Royalist, Sir Nicholas Kemeys. Cromwell, on his way to reduce Pembroke, demanded its surrender. When this was refused, he left Colonel Ewer and his regiment to reduce it. Ewer's four cannon quickly breached the walls, probably on the south side near Marten's Tower, where there is higher ground across the castle dell and where the present curtain wall is a late rebuild. As Ewer's men prepared to storm the breach, many of the garrison surrendered. Kemeys and the man who had originally betrayed the castle to him were killed, probably shot out of hand after the castle's fall. A plaque near the probable site of the

Right: The plaque within the lower bailey at Chepstow which commemorates Sir Nicholas Kemeys, killed during the Parliamentary attack and capture of the castle in 1648.

Below: The southern defences of the castle overlooking the dell. In the autumn of 1648, Parliamentarian troops fired across this natural valley until the curtain wall was breached, probably near Marten's Tower seen in the far distance in this view.

rming commemorates him. The 120
isoners, including many local Royalist
ntlemen, were imprisoned in Chepstow
urch, but later released.

*er Cromwell (1599-1658), painted by Robert Walker about 1649.
mwell was granted Chepstow Castle at the end of the Civil War when
lands of the marquess of Worcester were declared forfeit (By
mission of the National Portrait Gallery).*

romwell and After

AFTER THE WAR, the lands of the
marquess of Worcester were declared
feit and Chepstow castle was granted to
omwell. It now entered the last phase of its
story, as military barracks and place of
tention for political prisoners. Twice during
e war its defences, designed against
edieval siege warfare, had fallen rapidly to
nnon. Its whole southern face, from
arten's Tower to the barbican, was now
inforced to resist artillery. The towers were
led with earth, and a solid platform packed
th earth was added behind the curtain to
sorb the shock of cannon fire and to permit
e rapid movement of troops to any
reatened sector. The parapets of the wall
ere remodelled with rectangular openings
r muskets to enable the defenders to return
stile fire. The medieval towers were broken
rough at parapet level to make a unified
ae of defence. New stairs were provided up

to the parapets and the two inner walls of the
elegant rectangular tower in the south-east of
the upper bailey were demolished to make
way for stairs and the new fighting platform.

The exact date of these alterations is not
known with certainty. The Civil War garrison
had artillery, but the ease with which this was
neutralized by the Roundheads and the wall
breached suggest that it was mounted on the
medieval walls. Parliament spent £300 on the
castle in 1650, probably repairing siege
damage, and a further £500 was spent in
1662. These figures may indicate the broad
date of remodelling. The Civil War and
Restoration had left much undecided
politically, and the so-called 'Popish Plot'
(1678) — which owed much to local hostility
to the Roman Catholic Worcesters —
Monmouth's Rebellion (1685), and the
Revolution of 1688 still lay ahead. Garrisons
like Chepstow's, ensuring the stability of an
area, were still necessary.

The castle was also used for state prisoners.
Under Cromwell the High Anglican and
Royalist, Bishop Jeremy Taylor, a rather too
popular preacher and writer, was here in 1654-
55. The tradition that associates him with the
small sparse tower now called 'Jeremy Taylor's

Bishop Jeremy Taylor, author of Holy Living *and* Holy Dying, *who was
imprisoned at Chepstow in 1654-55 (By courtesy of the Warden and
Fellows of All Souls College, Oxford).*

Dungeon' is mere legend and it is more likely
that an important political prisoner of Taylor's
status would be given apartments like those
later occupied by Henry Marten.

Henry Marten, a left-wing Republican, was one of those who signed the death warrant of Charles I. He later quarrelled with Cromwell, whom he suspected of wishing to be king, and this perhaps saved his life at the Restoration, when most of his fellow regicides were executed. He was a prisoner here for twenty years, until his death in 1680 at the age of 78. It was a fairly comfortable captivity. Marten and his wife lived in the first-floor room of Marten's Tower, with their servants in the rooms above, and he was allowed to receive visitors and to visit the houses of neighbouring gentry. As late as 1799 the historian William Coxe met an old lady who lived in the castle and who remembered Marten's two former maidservants, who had told her about their master.

Henry Marten (1602-80), republican and regicide — one of those who signed the death warrant of King Charles I. Following the Restoration of Charles II in 1660, Marten was imprisoned at Chepstow for the last twenty years of his life. He spent his time in the tower which still bears his name (By courtesy of the National Portrait Gallery).

Chepstow remained a military garrison until 1690, when the remaining troops were withdrawn. The cannon were shipped to Chester, then presumably to Ireland for King William III's campaign against the Catholic James II. Parts including Marten's Tower, were still roofed and floored in the early nineteenth century and part of the hall block in the lower bailey housed a resident custodian until the 1950s, when the owner, Mr D.R. Lysaght, gave the State permanent guardianship of the castle. Both castle and town walls are now maintained by Cadw: Welsh Historic Monuments on behalf of the Secretary of State for Wales.

Chepstow Castle at the end of the eighteenth century, as painted by J.M.W. Turner (1775-1851). At the centre of the scene, Marten's Tower is still clearly roofed, and parts of the hall block in the lower bailey were also occupied at the time (By kind permission of the Courtauld Institute Galleries, London, Stephen Courtauld Collection, S.C. 1).

Chepstow Castle: A Tour-Guide

The Arrangement of The Guide

IT IS NOT THE PURPOSE OF THIS GUIDE to confine visitors to a rigid itinerary, since much of the pleasure of exploring a castle such as Chepstow rests in its ability to surprise the visitor with the unexpected, and to draw him or her to explore it further. The present tour-guide follows one of a number of possible routes from the entrance at the great gatehouse up through the castle to the barbican at the other end, but the various parts of the castle are labelled and with the help of the labels and of the coloured plan at the back of the guidebook the visitor should be able to find the relevant page for any part of the castle with ease. If time permits, a walk along the outside of the castle walls will help the interested visitor to understand and enjoy this fine castle.

The Outer Gatehouse: Chepstow 3 (1219-1245)

The visitor enters the castle through the twin-towered outer gatehouse, the approach to which was guarded by sets of cruciform arrowslits in each of its three levels. These were originally the only openings in its front face, for the large two- and three-light rectangular windows are sixteenth-century alterations. The scar of a wall on the left-hand flank of the entrance is all that is left of a barbican or defensive wall which, in conjunction with a drawbridge, covered the entrance from direct attack.

left: An aerial view of Chepstow seen from the east, looking towards the twin-towered outer gatehouse. Marten's Tower is to the right, and William fitz Osbern's hall-keep stands out clearly above the river cliff. The younger Marshal's outer gate remains the main entrance to the castle today.

A reconstruction drawing showing the outer gatehouse as it may have appeared when first built. The square holes near the top of the gate — visible in the adjacent aerial photograph — may have carried timbers to support a wooden fighting platform or hourd, as suggested here (Illustration by Terry Ball).

In the parapet at the top of the gatehouse are a series of squarish openings, which are seventeenth-century loops for firearms. Below them is a row of smaller square socket holes running right across the front of the gatehouse, showing that it was once crowned by a projecting wooden gallery or *hourd* from which archers could command the ground in front of the gate, and from which heavy stones or other missiles could be dropped on attackers. Two larger socket holes over the entrance arch suggest that the *hourd* was continued above the entrance as a pentice (penthouse) or projecting wooden turret.

The gate-passage, set between the two circular towers, was heavily defended. It had two portcullises — whose grooves can be seen in the side walls of the passage — with a pair of stout doors between. The present doors are replicas of the seventeenth-century or earlier originals, which are now on display in the castle exhibition (p. 29). In the underside of

The entrance passage through the gatehouse was protected by arrowloops, a pair of stout doors, two portcullises, and by 'murder holes' above.

the arch above are two circular 'murder-holes', through which missiles could be dropped on the heads of attackers, or water poured to douse a fire lit against the gate. More missiles could be dropped through the gap behind the arch across the front of the gatehouse at first-floor level. The gatehouse passage was further protected at close range by an arrowslit to the left.

The ground floor of the gatehouse contained the prison and the porter's lodge or guard room. The prison is in the north (right-hand) tower, and can be reached from inside the castle shop. It was a windowless cell with a narrow ventilation shaft in the wall. The door could only be opened from the jailor's room outside, where there is a small latrine.

The opposite gate tower (approached inside the castle from the lower bailey) is equipped at ground-floor level with arrowslits for defence. Only the foundations remain of the small square room behind the tower, which was probably a second porter's lodge, matching the jailor's room opposite.

The two upper floors of the gatehouse were reached by a spiral stair from the courtyard, whose door can be seen just next to the gatehouse proper. There were two rooms on the first floor and a single large room above. These were altered in Tudor times, with large rectangular windows supplementing the original arrowslits, and with fireplaces, some of which may replace medieval originals. The outer portcullis of the gate-passage was operated from the wall-walk and the inner portcullis from the now destroyed first-floor chamber, against whose east wall it rested when raised.

Once through the gate-passage, the visitor stands within a corner of the lower bailey (see p. 31). From the modern fence, straight ahead is Marshal's earlier curtain wall fronting the middle bailey, and to the left is the back of Marten's Tower, added by Roger Bigod III. The visitor must now turn to the right, entering the castle at the lower end of Roger Bigod III hall block, which now houses the ticket point and shop.

The Domestic Buildings of the Lower Bailey: Chepstow 4 (1270-1300)

THE WHOLE OF THE NORTHERN riverward side of the lower bailey is taken up by an elaborate block of buildings designed for the household of the baronial magnate, Roger Bigod III. Though the overall plan is complex, it is a highly functional answer to the problems of feeding and housing a large and intricate noble household. With a close social stratification, things had to be done in an ordered manner, each according to his rank. The block consists in effect of two adjoining ranges linked by a central 'cross-passage', itself designed to cope with the many cooks and waiters laden with dishes of food, or with jugs of wine and beer. Below the cross-passage was a large kitchen and — at the lower end — a three-storey chamber block, where this tour continues.

Servants laden with food and drink, destined for the great hall, are shown in this detail from the fourteenth-century Luttrell Psalter (By permission of the British Library, Additional Ms. 42130).

The domestic buildings ranged along the northern edge of the lower bailey. This complex but highly functional block of buildings was built by Roger Bigod III to accommodate his extensive household. The entrance porch with its battlemented top lies at the centre, with the more ruinous great hall to the left. The rear of the outer gatehouse appears to the right of the domestic block.

The East Chamber Block

THE LOWER FLOOR OF THIS chamber block is now occupied by the castle shop and ticket point. Originally, it was entered from the lower bailey by the same doorway used today. Just inside the entrance, a door on the immediate right led to the prison in the gatehouse tower (p. 20). Beyond this, on the left of the pair of small windows overlooking the river, someone — perhaps a prisoner — has scratched a cartoon-like figure of a man in late-medieval costume.

The two upper rooms of the block are best seen from outside the other modern door of the shop. These rooms provided chambers for officers of Bigod's household. Looking up, visitors will notice that each has a private latrine tucked into the riverside angle of the room, and may once have had a fireplace in the now rebuilt north wall. The first-floor room, originally reached by a wooden stair from the courtyard, is lit towards the bailey by what was initially a fine two-light window, like that on the floor above. There may have been a similar window in the opposite (riverside) wall, but this is now a rebuild. On the bailey side of the second floor, the chamber has a handsome two-light window with a quatrefoil head, but the present doorway next to it is a later insertion. The room may once have been reached by way of an external stair from a now vanished platform outside the riverward wall of the kitchen.

This example shows that there were architecturally fine windows at the lower end of the hall block, and demonstrates that the chambers in this area must have housed persons of some status (Illustration by Delyth Lloyd).

The Office of Marshal

Until the beginning of the fourteenth century, the lords of Chepstow Castle held the office of marshal. In origin, the marshal's role seems to have begun with the relatively lowly duty of caring for the king's horses. But gradually this developed into a more important military function and included keeping rolls of those who performed their military service. Other duties encompassed supervision of treasury expenditure and the maintenance of order in the palace.

One of the earliest known holders of this office was John fitz Gilbert, under King Henry I. He took the name of Marshal which his descendants continued to use, the most famous of which was his son William Marshal, under whom the office rapidly rose in importance. When the Marshal male line died out, the

The Kitchen

THE KITCHEN IS SITUATED between the east chamber block and the cross-passage. The wall separating it from the domestic chambers has vanished, but is now marked by a change in ground level near the outer wall of the modern shop. Because the two halves of Roger Bigod's range are set on different alignments, the kitchen is not a true rectangle, its wall with the service passage being at an angle.

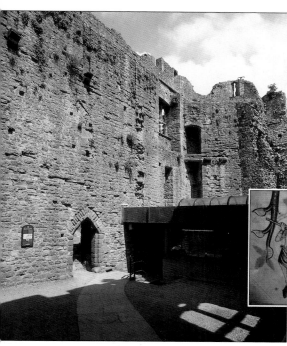

Above Left: *The kitchen within Roger Bigod's domestic block. This room would have been a tall single storey chamber with a central hearth. Beyond this, the east chamber block occupied the two storeys above the modern shop and probably housed officers of Bigod's household.*

Above: *Meat being roasted on an open kitchen hearth, depicted in a fourteenth-century manuscript illustration from the Luttrell Psalter (By permission of the British Library, Additional Ms. 42130).*

Medieval kitchens were usually, as here, tall buildings open to the roof to allow the escape of heat and smoke. The grooves of the wallpost timbers of the roof can be seen in the side walls. There was probably a large central cooking hearth in the centre of the room, and above this a louvre or ventilation turret within the roof. A small circular oven, of later date, survives in the north wall.

The wall of the kitchen towards the bailey is lit by a tall, two-light transomed window with a quatrefoil head, repaired in its lower part in modern times. The north wall — towards the river — has a similar window, plus a smaller one, but the latter was blocked up, probably in the sixteenth century, to make room for a fireplace and chimney. In turn, the fireplace was later blocked. A ground-floor doorway in the north wall now leads only to the river cliff, but would probably have led originally to a platform outside. From here a stair, overlooking the river, led up to the top floor of the adjacent chamber block.

ffice passed by marriage to the Bigods, earls of orfolk. From 1385/86 the holder of the office egan to be styled Earl Marshal; the office finally ecame hereditary in the house of Howard (the resent dukes of Norfolk) in 1672. It thus became ne of the highest and most powerful hereditary oyal offices of state.

eft: An early fourteenth-century manuscript illustration from the hroniques de France depicting the coronation of King Richard I. illiam Marshal the elder, in his role as marshal, participated in the remony by carrying the gold sceptre with the cross (By permission the British Library, Royal Ms. 16 G VI f. 347v).

elow: A section of the letter from King Henry III admitting Roger god III to the office of marshal of England, dated 4 May 1270. god's name also appears on later documents which record King dward I's decision to go to war against the Welsh prince, Llywelyn Gruffudd — his task, as marshal, was to muster the feudal army opyright: Public Record Office, Close Rolls, C54/87 m. 8d).

The Service Passage and Cellar

THE GROUND LEVEL ON WHICH Roger Bigod's domestic block stands falls away from west to east, so that whereas the part between the gatehouse and the service passage is at roughly the same level as this central cross point, the great hall beyond is somewhat higher. It is reached by a flight of service stairs from the middle of the passage.

Medieval halls of this date often had a central service door at their lower end, flanked by two further doors leading to a pair of rooms (buttery and pantry) where the food and drink were prepared for service at table. At Chepstow the stair from the service passage leads up to the central door, but there is an ingenious variation on the usual theme. The buttery and pantry were located in the middle tier of a three-storey block (see illustration), with a second pair of service rooms below (at the service passage level), and with a large private chamber above.

The tour continues at the far side of the passage, at the river end, where a stair on the left leads down to a large rib-vaulted cellar of three bays — the main storage point for the castle provisions. The dressed stone of the rib vaulting is of fine quality. An arched opening in the end wall overlooks the river and a small creek in the cliff face below. From this creek supplies could be hauled up by pulley or light crane from a small boat. In the early nineteenth century, the wooden door to the opening was still in place, as was an iron bracket in the floor for the pulley.

A platform overlooking the creek, reached from a landing halfway up the stairs, may also have been used for the hauling up of supplies. During one of the Civil War sieges the Royalists are said to have kept a small boat here for escape, but a Roundhead swam the river with a knife between his teeth, cut the rope holding the boat and towed it across the river, again using his teeth. When the Royalists rushed to escape, their boat had gone.

A reconstruction of Roger Bigod III's domestic block as it may have appeared about 1300. The buildings are seen from the riverward side, with the chamber block and kitchen to the left. The service passage, with its access to the river and cellar, appears at the centre, and the great hall lies to the top right (Illustration by Terry Ball).

12 *Barbican* — The upper end of the castle is protected by a barbican or outer defence, whose curtain wall and corner towers have batteries of arrowslits to repel attackers (pp. 43-5).

11 *Corner Tower* — This square tower of the upper ward contains domestic accommodation for persons of high status (p. 42).

10 *Upper Bailey* — The eleventh-century great tower was flanked by two stone walled baileys, the upper and middle wards. Chepstow was unusual in being walled in stone at this date, when most castles were of earth and timber (p. 42).

9 *Great Tower* — Built by William fitz Osbern before his death in 1071, the hall keep is closely similar to eleventh-century building in Normandy. Entry was by way of a round-headed Norman doorway with a chip-carved decorated head (pp. 4-5, 37-41).

8 *Middle Bailey* — Originally this was the eastern outer wall of the castle, fronted by a ditch subsequently filled in. William Marshal's two round mural towers are among the earliest examples in this country of this method of defence (pp. 35-6).

4 *Lower Bailey* — Added to the castle by the sons of William Marshal, between 1219 and 1245. Before that date the castle ended at the wall with the two round towers fronting the Middle Bailey (pp. 8-9, 31).

3 *Musket Loops* — The walls along this side of the castle were strengthened in the seventeenth century with earth filled platforms, designed to resist artillery fire, and the parapets were looped for musketry. It was probably here that the walls were breached by Parliament's guns in the second Civil War siege (pp. 14, 31).

2 *Marten's Tower* — Built as a suite of self-contained apartments for Roger Bigod III, 1285-93, the tower was for many years the prison of Henry Marten, one of the men who signed the death warrant of Charles I (pp. 32-4).

(Illustration by Terry Ball)

26

A Bird's-Eye View of Chepstow Castle from the South-East

with notes on some of the principal features

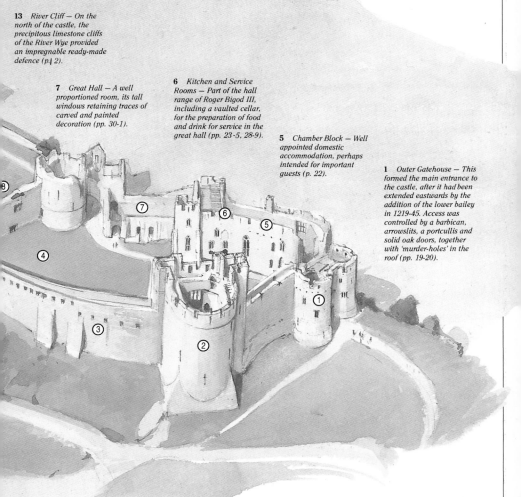

13 *River Cliff — On the north of the castle, the precipitous limestone cliffs of the River Wye provided an impregnable ready-made defence (p. 2).*

7 *Great Hall — A well proportioned room, its tall windows retaining traces of carved and painted decoration (pp. 30-1).*

6 *Kitchen and Service Rooms — Part of the hall range of Roger Bigod III, including a vaulted cellar, for the preparation of food and drink for service in the great hall (pp. 23-5, 28-9).*

5 *Chamber Block — Well appointed domestic accommodation, perhaps intended for important guests (p. 22).*

1 *Outer Gatehouse — This formed the main entrance to the castle, after it had been extended eastwards by the addition of the lower bailey in 1219-45. Access was controlled by a barbican, arrowslits, a portcullis and solid oak doors, together with 'murder-holes' in the roof (pp. 19-20).*

At the top of the stairs there is a double cupboard of dressed stone, which may have held supplies of knives, table napkins and the like needed by the waiters. Here, at the end of the service passage, the cupboard was

The two cupboards at the top of the cellar stairs in the service passage, where servants could collect knives or table linen for diners in the great hall.

accessible to all the serving staff, unlike those cupboards in the adjacent service rooms for the use of the butler and upper waiters who served the high table in the great hall with wine and choice meats on silver and plate. Next to the cupboard (to the right) is the entrance to a roomy two-seater latrine discharging into the river below.

The Service Rooms

THE LOWER TWO service rooms are situated either side of the stair up to the hall. That nearest the bailey is an L-shaped room with two pairs of cupboards of dressed stone. The cupboard to the right is open, the second lies blocked behind the replica wooden doors. They must have been for the storage of fine wine or silver plate, and the siting of this room between the kitchens and the service stairs to the great hall suggests that it may have been where the food for the high table and more favoured guests was plated and arranged for the table. A tableau has been installed illustrating how the room might have looked when in use.

The second of the pair of these lower service rooms lies back around the corner, near the head of the stairs leading to the cellar. It has only recently been unblocked and exposed. Although very small, it may have

A flight of steps at the end of the service passage leads down to a large vaulted cellar. It was the main storage area in the castle, and supplies could be hauled up directly from boats anchored in the river below. A small room at the top of the stairs may have been used as an office by the clerk or cellarer who checked the movements of supplies to and from the stores.

functioned as an office for the clerk or cellarer who checked the stores of food and drink leaving the cellar and arriving by boat, preventing pilfering and theft. Again, the room is now shown as it may have been when in use, with a figure of the steward checking the cellarer's accounts.

This fourteenth-century manuscript illustration from the Luttrell Psalter shows the plating of food ready to be served at high table. At Chepstow, as elsewhere, such tasks are likely to have taken place away from the kitchen, in one of the adjacent service rooms (By permission of the British Library, Additional Ms. 42130).

The two upper service rooms are reached from the top of the stairs leading from the cross-passage. These rooms now house an exhibition illustrating the history of the castle and of medieval fortification. The doorways which led to the buttery on one side and the pantry on the other are located at the 'lower' end of Roger Bigod's hall, either side of a central door from the stairs. They were separated from the hall proper by a timber screen (see below). All three doorways were once decorated with pairs of sculptured human heads, the sadly battered remains of the central pair still surviving. Traces of

One of the sadly battered sculptured heads which once adorned all three doorways at the top of the service stairs.

medieval painted decoration remain around the right-hand door, leading to what was probably the pantry.

Inside, the pantry now houses figures of the four main builders of the castle, with models of the site as it was in each phase. From this room, a spiral stair led up to a small chamber over the entrance porch, perhaps the lodging of a household official. The pantry was originally almost square, and a solid cross-wall separated it from the service passage beyond. This cross-wall was removed when the service block was in use as cottages. In the medieval centuries, there would have been no floor within the passage area (the section which now links the two halves of the exhibition), which was the upper part of the cross-passage below. But in order to make space for exhibits, and to permit circulation, the cottage-period floor level has been retained, with the result that the heads of arches at either end of the passageway now project through the floor.

The second of the two service rooms was probably the buttery, where beer and wine was kept awaiting service at table. The stub of the cross-wall, once separating it from the passage, can be seen in this room. On the far wall, a small wooden door replaces a medieval original whose hinges survive. The door covers a sink or drain, which may have been for washing the drinking vessels. Originally, the floor would have continued to the end wall, but has been stopped short to make room for the modern spiral stair.

The private chamber block above the service rooms was originally reached by the spiral stair from the lower end of the hall, via a door at first-floor level in the left-hand (riverward) end of the hall wall. Visitors may care to use the modern spiral stair.

The chamber, or camera (which now houses an exhibition on the Civil War), has a very large medieval fireplace and was clearly the private apartment of someone of high rank, perhaps even Roger Bigod himself. The late medieval doors of the outer gatehouse are also now exhibited in this room.

These very fine late medieval doors once belonged to the outer gatehouse, and can now be seen on display in the great private chamber above the service rooms. The present outer gatehouse doors are replicas.

The Great Hall

THE STAIRS UP FROM the cross-passage also provided the service entrance to Roger Bigod's great hall. At the head of the stairs there was a further passage running across the width of the block and separated from the hall proper by a timber screen (see illustration pp. 24-5). The hall itself was once a very fine and well proportioned room, but is now sadly ruined.

The grand entrance into the hall was by way of a two-storey porch entered from the bailey outside, the external doorway to which is currently (1991) blocked. Inside, however, the vaulted ground floor of the porch retains some of its original medieval painted decoration, with two painted armorial shields hung by painted ribbons from painted nails over the door leading into the hall.

Roger Bigod's great hall seen from the lower bailey. This once fine room was originally entered through the two-storey porch to the right, and was lit by two tall and richly-decorated windows on this courtyard side.

In this late thirteenth-century manuscript illustration, a nobleman, his family and guests, eat at high table, whilst musicians entertain them. Roger Bigod, as one of the most powerful men at the court of King Edward I, would have dined and been entertained on a lavish scale. Indeed, he is known to have played host to the king at Chepstow for several days in 1285 (By permission of the British Library, Additional Ms. 28162, f. 10v).

Once through the porch, those entering also found themselves in the service passage at the lower end of the hall.

Beyond the position of the medieval timber screen, the hall was a tall single storey room, originally open to a roof of timber. It was lit by two tall windows, now sadly ruined, in the wall towards the courtyard. They are

A detail of the finely-carved floral motifs on one of the windows which look out from the great hall to the lower bailey. A similar decoration can be seen around the window in the chapel in Marten's Tower.

decorated with finely-carved floral motifs, like those on the window of the chapel in Marten's Tower (p. 33). Around the windows, traces of the medieval painted decoration survive, with the cream surface picked out with red lines to imitate blocks of expensive squared freestone. There were also similar windows in the opposite wall, which overlooked the river, but these are now blocked and largely hidden.

The dais, with the high table, would have been below the plain (westerly) end wall. Here the lord and his guests would have sat facing the fine two-light window, now blocked with brickwork, situated above the level of the screen in the gable of the opposite wall. A door in the upper angle (north-west) of the hall leads to a small square annexe overlooking the river, which in turn led to a spiral stair. This may have been intended to lead up to a chamber above the upper end of the hall which was never built.

Opposite this point, there is a gap in the wall of the great hall, through which visitors may care to progress to the next point on the tour.

The Lower Bailey

THE LOWER BAILEY was added to the earlier castle by the sons of William Marshal between 1219 and 1245. From the middle of its courtyard all four main periods of the castle's history can be seen. The tall rectangular shape of the eleventh-century hall-keep (Chepstow 1) can be seen straight ahead, closing the view. Nearer, at the upper end of the bailey, are the early thirteenth-century curtain wall and towers of Chepstow 2. Until the addition of the lower bailey to the castle, this formed its eastern outer wall. The outer gatehouse (the main entrance) is part of Chepstow 3. To the left and right respectively are the private rooms of Roger Bigod III in Marten's Tower, and his great hall and domestic buildings described above.

The east curtain of the bailey, between the gatehouse and Marten's Tower, is of the same date as the gatehouse, but all save the lowest part near the gate was totally reconstructed when Marten's Tower was built. It has dumb-bell shaped arrowloops like those in the tower.

The south curtain, from Marten's Tower to the junction with the middle bailey, is particularly thick and massive. The outer part is on roughly the line of the medieval curtain wall, but the whole structure in its present

Seventeenth-century musket loops in the parapet of the lower bailey (Illustration by Delyth Lloyd).

form is seventeenth century. It has a row of squarish loops for firearms in the parapet (best seen from outside), and an earth filling behind. The large rear wall tracing the interior of the bailey may be a later rebuild, perhaps of the eighteenth or nineteenth century.

Marten's Tower

MARTEN'S TOWER IS ENTERED from the bailey through a pointed doorway protected by a portcullis outside its door. The two doorways into the tower from the wall-walk of the curtain wall were similarly protected and the tower could thus be shut off and separately defended in case of need. The wooden door to the tower, probably of late medieval date and with three triangular peepholes, is still in place, as is one on the first floor. The stone slab in the grass outside the door marks the position of the castle well.

Main Picture: *The rear face of Marten's Tower faces on to the lower bailey; the large windows were added in the sixteenth century.*

Inset: *The spacious suite of accommodation afforded by Marten's Tower would probably have been used by Roger Bigod himself. This fourteenth-century manuscript shows servants dressing their lord, by the fire in a private chamber (By permission of the British Library, Royal Ms. 2 B VII, f. 72v).*

The tower was still roofed and inhabited in the early years of the nineteenth century.

The tower is a massive D-shaped structure, rounded externally but with a flat rear face towards the bailey. On the outside, it is protected by two massive pyramidal spurs of masonry — a defensive device seen on a number of castles of this date in south Wales, which served to protect it from attack by battering ram or undermining, for it is set at one of the most exposed points of the castle's defences.

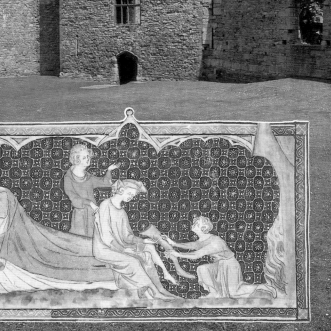

...ur buttresses, designed to strengthen Marten's Tower against siege ...gines or to protect it from undermining. Such buttresses occur in a ...mber of other late thirteenth- and early fourteenth-century castles in ...uth Wales.

Internally, it provides a suite of ...ccommodation for the lord of the castle ...rranged in three storeys over an unlit ...asement. The work of Roger Bigod III, it was ...nder way by 1287 and completed in 1293. A ...piral stair to the left of the entrance leads to ...he upper floors. The ground floor, above the ...indowless basement, was military rather ...han domestic, with three arrowloops set in ...eep recesses. These each had an extra ...ircular hole cut through their centre in the ...eventeenth century for use with firearms.

Climbing the spiral stairs to the landing on ...he floor above, the visitor will notice similar ...oops at this level, one enlarged into a window ...n the sixteenth century. Its rear wall is lit by ...a large rectangular seventeenth-century ...indow of wood, though the fine stonework ...f the recess suggests that it replaced a ...xteenth-century window of stone, like that ...n the floor above. From the landing, within ...he window recess, the portcullis of the ...ntrance arch was operated. Traces of the ...riginal wall decoration, in red and yellow, ...an be seen on the adjacent wall. Two ...ectangular fireplaces are inserted on one side ...f the room. The larger one, probably late ...iedieval, is the earlier. There is a latrine in ...ie corner of the room.

The stairs continue up to the second floor which is of a more domestic quality and at this height from the ground, larger windows could be provided at little risk. The two lancet windows have seats in their recesses and there is a medieval fireplace — with a later head — and a latrine. A large sixteenth-century window has been inserted in the rear wall. At this level, the tower is entered from the wall-walk of the curtain wall through the pair of flanking turrets. Each entry is protected by a portcullis.

In the north turret, the circular stair continues up to a small private chapel where the lord and his immediate retainers would hear mass. There would have been at least one larger chapel elsewhere in the castle for the rest of its inhabitants. The arch of the east window of the chapel is richly carved with flower motifs like those on the windows of Roger Bigod's hall, though the actual tracery

The floral decoration of the chapel windows in Marten's Tower can be paralled closely in Roger Bigod's great hall.

The battlements on Marten's Tower, where the carved figures can be matched with other castles of the period in north Wales and northern England (Illustration by John Banbury).

has vanished. The decoration is also similar to the west front of Tintern Abbey, whose rebuilding was funded by Bigod. On each side of the chapel is a lancet window with a semi-circular seat below for the priest. By the right hand seat is a *piscina* or small sink for washing the sacred vessels. Rather less usual in a chapel, though not without parallel, is the slot in the floor for the portcullis closing off the wall-walk below which, when raised, would have stood in front of the altar.

From the chapel, the stair rises to the roof. The battlements are complete, each merlon having an arrowslit in a shouldered 'Caernarfon' arch (so called from its frequent use in Edward I's great north Welsh castle) and a carved human figure on its crest — a sort of garrison in stone. There are rather similar figures on Edward I's Eagle Tower at Caernarfon Castle, at York and in several castles in Northumbria. Nearly all belong to the early years of the fourteenth century. The two flanking turrets rise up to a higher level at the rear corners of the roof, the north turret having a battlemented platform. The slot for the portcullis which shut off Marten's Tower from the south curtain wall can be seen in the turret on the side away from the stair.

A portcullis slot in Marten's tower. Each doorway in the tower had its own portcullis, and it could be shut off and separately defended in c of need.

The roof was originally low pitched, but it w heightened in the sixteenth century and an extra storey formed in the roof space. A fireplace of this phase can be seen, and the wall of the heightened roof blocks an arrows near the head of the stairs.

From outside the castle it can be seen tha the topmost part of the tower, with the stringcourse and battlements, is constructed in slightly different masonry from the rest, th neat coursed blocks being replaced by a mor irregular pale limestone. After Bigod's death in 1306 money was spent in completing and probably in roofing his unfinished work and may be that these upper parts belong to thes years.

The Middle Bailey

THE MIDDLE BAILEY was part of William fitz Osbern's eleventh-century castle, and outside the castle part of the stone curtain wall of this period can be seen, together with a small postern gate. However, before progressing to the interior, there is much to note in the outer face of the east curtain wall.

Middle Bailey — East Curtain: Chepstow 2 (c. 1200)

THE UPPER END of the lower bailey is closed by the curtain wall built by William Marshal the elder sometime after his marriage in 1189, though the exact date is unknown. Until the lower bailey was added, this was the outer wall of the castle, fronted by a wide ditch now filled in. In Tudor times a range of two-storey buildings, now demolished, was built against the wall. This accounts for the fireplaces now visible in the wall face and for the later doorways cut into the sides of the tower at ground-floor level.

The wall is of limestone quarried from the rock on which the castle stands, with dressings of Dundry stone from the quarries outside Bristol. It is one of the very first examples in Britain of the new military technique which was developed — probably in northern France — towards the end of the twelfth century, which later came to be characteristic of the medieval castle. The two circular towers command the area in front of the curtain wall, which could be swept with cross fire from the arrowslits in wall and towers. Rather similar defences had been used in late Roman times. It is sometimes thought that returning crusaders may have brought the idea back from the Byzantine east, but it is more probable that westerners developed it at home, perhaps taught by surviving Roman forts and town walls.

The fourth-century town walls and towers at the Roman town of Caerwent. Late Roman defences such as these, in Britain and France, may have influenced the castle builders of the early thirteenth century.

William Marshal's curtain wall and towers, strengthening the then outer face of the castle against attack. This is one of the earliest known examples of this type of medieval fortification.

The gateway through the curtain (to the right) is a simple pointed arch, closed by a pair of doors probably of late medieval date, with triangular peepholes. There is no portcullis, emphasizing the early date. The sides of two doors can be seen inside the wall, north (right) of the arch, suggesting that there was a guardroom here.

Flanking the gate is a round tower with two later ground-floor doors cut through its walling. It was turned into a kitchen in the sixteenth century and an oven and fireplace are visible inside it. In 1800 it was still known as the Old Kitchen. At the same time as the kitchen was inserted, the original door in the rear wall was blocked and a window put in above it.

The tower has three storeys, the bottom two marked externally by a chamfered offset of dressed stone, as in contemporary French castles. There are arrowslits at each level, also of dressed stone. The upper floors were reached from the wall-walk and thence by a spiral stair, there being no access from the ground floor. The stair walls are of dressed stone retaining some of the masons' marks which served as a form of quality control, enabling the work of individual masons to be recognized (these are now only accessible by ladder). Two more arrowslits, now blocked, can be seen in the face of the curtain wall between the two towers.

The second round tower stood at the outer angle of the castle until the wall of the middle bailey was added against it. It would originally have matched the other tower, with three

Details like the horizontal string courses of once fine ashlar on the exterior of this tower show that William Marshal's castle building had links with comtemporary military architecture in France.

storeys each marked by a chamfered external string course, though little trace of these no remains inside the castle, where they can on be seen at second-floor level. Each storey wa provided with arrowslits. Externally, it has a thickened sloping base, the better to resist t effects of siege engines and mining. It has been much altered, with a ground-floor doo of Tudor date cut through an original arrowslit and a domed vault and a latrine inserted inside. Its upper floors are largely obscured by the thickened seventeenth-century rampart, and when this was built, th tower was cut through to give direct access between the wall-walks of the two baileys, a the first floor of the tower filled in with eart

Middle Bailey — Other Features

WITHIN THE MIDDLE BAILEY, apart from fitz Osbern's eleventh-century work in the southern curtain, the remainder of the curtain wall was built in the thirteenth century, when the rounded tower mid way along it was added. After the Civil War it wa thickened with loops for firearms, an earth ramp and a heavily buttressed rear wall.

In the seventeenth century, following the Civil War, the outer wall of the middle bailey was thickened and the tower halfway along its leng was filled with earth to resist cannon fire during any future attack (Illustration by Delyth Lloyd).

The rounded tower, three storeys high, has cruciform arrowslits like those in the outer gatehouse, with which it is contemporary. Ahead, the ward is overlooked by William fitz Osbern's hall-keep. The northern side of this bailey, along the cliff edge, is bounded by a slight wall of uncertain date.

The Great Tower: Chepstow 1 (1067-1075), with Later Additions

UNTIL THE BUILDING OF Roger Bigod's hall block in the lower bailey, the great hall of the castle was in this tower.

The lord feasting his followers in hall was a powerful social symbol in the Middle Ages. The lord sat with his family and noble guests on a dais or platform at the high end, with his followers ranged at tables down the length of the hall. Many schools and colleges retain similar seating arrangements today. Here at Chepstow, as was often the case, the hall was on the first floor, with the ground floor serving as a basement. An upper floor was added above these in the thirteenth century, in two stages.

William fitz Osbern's powerful hall-keep (the great tower), which is the earliest datable secular stone building in Britain. Its siting high above the Wye cliffs was no doubt pure Norman propaganda.

Externally, the great tower is a rectangular, almost box-like, structure. Each of its wall faces is divided up by a series of tall shallow pilaster buttresses. The building stone used is itself of some interest. Several bands of red tile, probably robbed from the ruins of the Roman town of Caerwent, a few miles to the west, are particularly distinctive.

37

This is a late Roman building technique, copied from surviving Roman ruins in France (where it is especially common) or Britain. The small squarish blocks of coursed stone used elsewhere in the walling may also be from Caerwent, but the much larger blocks of soft yellowish stone, used particularly in some of the buttresses, are Triassic sandstone from the Sudbrook area, south-west of Chepstow.

The tower was entered from the middle bailey by way of an external wooden stair leading to a rectangular doorway with rounded head, raised well above ground level, in the east wall. There is a sloping plinth below the doorway, but the terrace and steps now seen below this are part of the seventeenth-century thickening of the curtain. The rounded head of the doorway has 'chip-carved' decoration of a type used in eleventh-century Normandy. The doorway gave access to the ground floor, possibly with wooden steps leading down into the interior. From a landing inside the doorway, a stair to the left led diagonally up in the thickness of the wall to the first-floor hall.

The entrance to the great tower. The circular head above the doorway has familiar Norman chip-carved decoration. The first-floor decorative blind arcading and 'bull's-eye' windows can be seen beyond.

The present entry to the tower is through ground level doorway cut through the wall near one corner of the riverward side. This reuses some of the big blocks of yellow sandstone from the original walls, but is probably a latter addition designed to give easier access to the ground floor.

The ground level inside the tower now slopes down from the upper end, the origina round headed door is situated well above th ground. It is possible that the floor may initially have been level with this door, in which case it must have been lowered when the present access doorway was inserted. Th lowest courses of the walling inside the low end of the tower are less regular than the neater squared masonry above, and may hav been foundation courses, showing that the floor level inside the tower was originally higher.

The interior of William fitz Osbern's hall-block. The ground floor wa basement with the hall itself on the floor above. Subsequent additio by the sons of William Marshal and Roger Bigod III raised the grea tower to three storeys.

The ground floor itself is lit by three smal round-headed windows in the safe riverside wall. This is much thinner than the opposite wall which faced the enemy. It is clear, from the large central beam hole in each end wal that a row of wooden posts originally ran down the middle of this room bearing a longitudinal beam across which the main timbers of the upper floor were laid. The ho for these floor joists can be seen in turn alo the length of both side walls.

On the first floor, the hall is a large rectangular room, originally lit on the riverward side by a series of round-headed windows, though all save one at the east end were blocked up and replaced by larger windows in the thirteenth century. The entry door is in one of the lower (south-east) angles, and the upper (west) wall and the southern wall have blind arcades of round-headed niches, some of which retain clear traces of painted or stuccoed decoration. Those in the south wall are mostly blocked and are not easy to identify. One of these blocked ones in the southern wall is broader, and was probably a fireplace. However, its pointed head shows it

to be thirteenth-century and not part of the original eleventh-century hall, which may have been warmed by braziers. To the left of this blocked firplace, the keen-eyed visitor may spot a small sculptured panel with human figures. This is a piece of reused Roman religious sculpture, probably from Caerwent, set here by the builders of the hall. One of the capitals of the arcade in the upper wall has a rope-cabled border, and may also be a reused Roman piece.

A Roman sculpture, possibly from Caerwent, reused in the Norman stonework of the great tower.

reconstruction of the great tower as it may have appeared in the time f William fitz Osbern. The upper end of the hall is shown artitioned off, forming a private chamber for the ord and his family (Illustration by Terry Ball).

The upper end of the hall would probably have been partitioned off by a wooden screen to form a chamber, or private withdrawing room for the lord and his family. A tall, narrow door in the riverward wall would have led to an external wooden stair, itself giving private access to the room. High in the upper end wall are two round 'bull's-eye' windows, and originally there may have been a third.

In the early thirteenth century, the sons of William Marshal remodelled the interior of the great tower to improve the standard of accommodation.

To begin with, the hall on the first floor was probably extended, doing away with the screened off chamber at the upper end. To replace this chamber, a new one was built above the upper third (west) of the extended hall. Its east wall was supported on a large and elegantly moulded arch spanning the hall, on the line of the presumed earlier timber partition, and decorated with a version

A reconstruction of the great tower as it may have appeared in the middle of the thirteenth century, after the additions made by the younger Marshals (Illustration by Terry Ball).

of the currently fashionable 'dog-tooth' ornament. The ends of this arch can be seen against the side walls, though the arch itself has fallen.

The tomb effigy of Gilbert Marshal, which lies near that of his father in the Temple Church in the City of London. Gilbert succeeded in the lordship of Chepstow in 1234 and undertook an energetic programme of building through to his death even years later (see p. 44). The modifications to the great tower no doubt continued at this time.

All the original windows at this first-floor level, save one, were now replaced by two-light windows, with quatrefoil tracery in the heads and finely moulded rear arches. The window at the upper end, which would have lit the high table, is larger, with a pair of two-light windows (parts of the tracery are now missing) under a moulded arch. The new upper chamber was lit by a pair of windows in the north (riverward) wall, similar to those in the hall below.

Between 1292 and 1300, the chamber over the upper third (west) of the hall was extended by Roger Bigod to form an upper storey to the whole of the great tower. Today, however, virtually all of the long south wall, and much of the east wall, have disappeared. In the north and east walls are pairs of windows with shouldered 'Caernarfon' arches, set in arched recesses. Holes for grills or, hinged shutters, can be seen in the sides of the windows, which use purple-red sandstone in place of the cream-coloured Dundry limestone of the earlier phase. An interesting roof corbel, in the form of the sculptured head of a bearded man, survives in one of the lower (north-east) angles of the tower.

Detail of a roof corbel of about 1292-1300 in the north-east angle of the great tower. Although sadly weathered, it is in the form of a sculptured head of a bearded man.

The battlements of the tower were reached by a stair in the north wall. This led from a door situated in the side of a window and set in a corbelled out buttress-like projection and a thickening of the wall rising diagonally from this, carried on a moulded half arch. Originally access to the battlements had been from the stair in the lower corner of the tower. Today, parts of the battlements survive in the west end wall, pierced by long, plunging, cross shaped arrowloops.

The Gallery and Upper Bailey

THE NARROW PASSAGEWAY between the face of the great tower and the river cliff was protected by an arcaded gallery. The upper and lower ends were closed by battlemented walls each with an entrance arch, though that at the upper end is now destroyed. Along the river cliff is a series of round-headed arches, now partly blocked, overlooking the river. The defensible parapet above was reached by the first-floor doorway from the great tower. The gallery served two purposes. It increased the security of the castle by helping to divide it into a series of self-contained compartments, each capable of separate defence. It also gave an observation platform from which shipping on the river could be controlled. The arches may have led to a wooden gallery for this purpose above the river.

A gallery runs alongside the great tower, and effectively separated the upper and middle baileys, dividing them into self-contained compartments. The row of now partly blocked arches probably served as vantage points, to observe and control shipping on the river.

The gallery leads to the upper bailey. From this, there is a good view of the west face of fitz Osbern's keep (great tower), the bailey being one of the pair of stone-walled wards flanking this keep. Part of the original eleventh-century curtain can be seen on the outer face of the south curtain wall, but most of the present curtain is thirteenth century, strengthened with an added earthen bank and musket loops after the Civil War.

When this was done, the inner walls of the rectangular south-west tower of the upper bailey were demolished so that it could be incorporated within these new defences. Its original external windows were blocked and fitted with musket loops similar to those in the parapet of the curtain wall (the filling of one window has since disappeared). The thickened parapet was continued across the tower, with access steps being added at one end.

In its original form, the south-west tower contained domestic accommodation of high quality, with a single lofty upper room, no doubt reached by an external stair, over a low cellar. The five surviving windows, with finely

The south-west corner tower of the upper bailey. Added to the castle in the first half of the thirteenth century, it contained domestic accommodation of high quality.

moulded rear arches, are of dressed blocks of Dundry limestone. One side of the ground-floor doorway into the cellar survives near the archway through to the barbican. This may have been the *camera comitisse* — a private sitting room for the countess and her ladies — mentioned in a thirteenth-century document. It was probably the first part of the additions to the castle by the younger Marshals, carried out soon after their father's death in 1219. The battlements of the tower remain, those on the outer sides being pierced with arrowloops. A line of socket holes in the walling below them may be for a wooden gallery or *hourd*.

The south-west tower in the upper bailey may have been the camera comitisse — a private sitting room for the countess and her ladies — which is mentioned in a thirteenth-century document. This detail from a fourteenth-century French manuscript shows a lady in her private apartment or sitting room (By courtesy of the National Library of Wales, Ms. 5016 D, f. 3r).

The Barbican

THE ARCHWAY IN THE curtain of the upper bailey, defended by a pair of doors, but no portcullis, leads across a modern bridge over a partly rock-cut ditch to a barbican — a heavily-defended outer ward added to this vulnerable face of the castle by the younger Marshals to protect it from direct attack. Until the building of this barbican, the

The barbican was added at the upper end of the castle, by the younger Marshals, to strengthen the defences on the western perimeter.

ditch was the outer defence of the castle. The bridge rests on an earlier pier (perhaps sixteenth century) which has replaced the original medieval bridge.

The defences curve round in an arc from the rectangular south-west tower of the upper bailey to the river cliff, with a circular tower guarding the angle and giving covering fire to the area outside the curtain. At the west end are the arch and tower of the upper gatehouse. This fine piece of military architecture really needs to be seen both from inside and outside (see photograph p. 45). This account therefore describes both the interior and (for the interested visitor with time to view the castle from the outside) external features.

Curtain wall and corner tower of the upper bailey join in a way which shows that the curtain was built against the tower and is therefore later than it. The curtain had parapets to front and rear and could have been used to defend the ditch even if attackers had forced the barbican. A round-headed postern gate in the ditch bottom is now blocked.

The South-West Tower

THIS TOWER IS OF THREE STOREYS over an unlit basement. It is open at the back, and the rear wall may originally have been of timber. Access to the upper floors was by a circular stair. Each floor is equipped with a battery of cruciform arrowslits in purple-red sandstone, though a limited supply of Dundry stone was still in stock and was used for the inner arches of the ground-floor arrowslits and for the bases of the first-floor slits. There are no domestic fittings — fireplaces or latrines — and the tower is purely a military work, designed to meet attackers with a lethal barrage from its archers. The original battlements were remodelled to house cannon in the seventeenth century. In the early nineteenth century the tower was filled with earth and the rear blocked with a stone wall, but these have now been removed.

From the outside it can be seen that the lower part of the tower is built against the curtain wall in a straight joint, whereas — in the upper part — tower and curtain are built as one. This shows that the curtain wall had already been built for part of its height when it was decided to add the tower to improve the flanking fire and strengthen this vulnerable angle of the castle, and that, originally, only a simple curtain wall was intended.

Left: *An artist's impression of how the south-west tower of the barbican may have appeared. The rear face to the tower was of timber, and its walls housed batteries of arrowslits to defend this angle of the castle (Illustration by Chris Ravenhill).*
Below: *The south-west tower of the barbican as it appears today.*

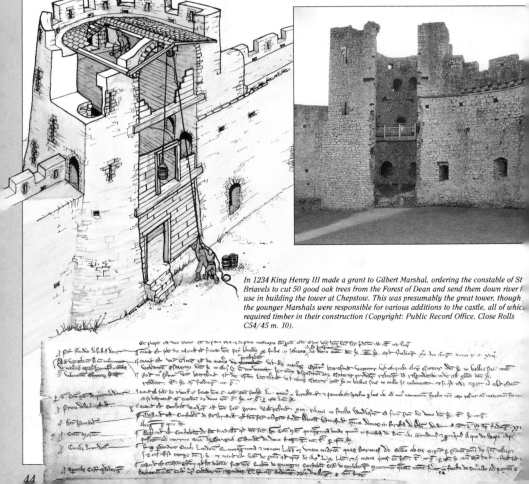

In 1234 King Henry III made a grant to Gilbert Marshal, ordering the constable of St Briavels to cut 50 good oak trees from the Forest of Dean and send them down river for use in building the tower at Chepstow. This was presumably the great tower, though the younger Marshals were responsible for various additions to the castle, all of which required timber in their construction (Copyright: Public Record Office, Close Rolls C54/45 m. 10).

Curtain Wall and Upper Gatehouse

FROM THE SOUTH-WEST TOWER, the curtain continues round to the upper gatehouse. It has a battery of four arrowslits, one of which has been blocked by the late thirteenth-century addition to the gatehouse. The battlements survive, and are equipped with more arrowslits, whilst a line of holes on the outside suggest that at one time there was a projecting wooden fighting-gallery or hourd.

Below: The barbican, originally built by the younger Marshals, was strengthened by Roger Bigod with the addition of an upper gatehouse at the end of the thirteenth century.

Right: The upper floor of the barbican gatehouse, viewed from the wall-walk.

Access to the upper rooms of the gate tower was by way of the spiral stair in the south-west tower and then along the wall-walk of the curtain. Corbels on the rear face of the curtain support a rear parapet added to protect this access and partly to enable the wall to be defended even if the gate-passage had been forced by the enemy. Attackers would thus find themselves ambushed by archery fire from the rear face of the curtain.

In its original form, the upper gateway consisted of a simple pointed arch through the curtain with a segmental arch over the passageway, but no portcullis. This was felt to be a weak spot in the castle defences and one of the first tasks of Roger Bigod's military engineers was to strengthen the entrance with a tower of three storeys added to the outside of the curtain about 1270. The passageway is defended by a portcullis, the grooves of which stopped short of ground level. There are also two slits in the stone-vaulted roof of the passage, through which missiles could be dropped on the heads of attackers trying to force the gate-passage.

The door from the curtain led into the upper floor of the gatehouse, from which the first-floor room, from which the portcullis operated, would have been reached by a wooden stair. The gatehouse is well equipped on the outside with cruciform arrowslits like those in the Roger Bigod hall block and there are windows in the safe rear wall in each of the floors above the entrance passage, with a two-light window in the uppermost one.

The walls of the barbican show particularly well the horizontal rows of socket holes into which the wooden scaffolding used by the medieval builders was secured. Other examples can be seen elsewhere in the castle.

The Port Wall

MEDIEVAL CHEPSTOW, SET IN A LOOP OF THE WYE, seems to have had no defences until the end of the thirteenth century, when Roger Bigod III enclosed its landward side with a stone wall 1,200 yards (1,097m) in length, enclosing an area of some 130 acres (53ha), and equipped with a series of semi-circular projecting towers and a gatehouse. This wall, known locally as the Port (i.e. town) Wall ran from the western end of the castle by the upper barbican across the neck of the promontory to meet the Wye again on the flat ground beyond the present railway.

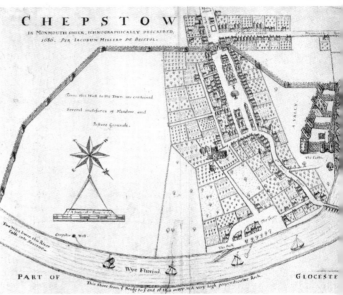

Jacob Millerd's map of Chepstow, dated 1686, shows the castle, the town and the full extent of the town walls, set in a loop in the River Wye (By kind permission of Newport Borough Libraries).

The town occupied only a very small part of this, around the big main square and the church, most of the enclosed area being orchards and fields well into the last century. Within the walls, as the visitor will notice, the streets of Chepstow slope quite sharply upwards from the bridge and castle towards the square and the town gate. The large area enclosed is explained by the way in which any line of defences on this sloping ground would have been overlooked within bowshot by higher ground outside the walls. It was therefore necessary to align the walls along the crest of the slope.

Visitors can reach the Port Wall by walking up the broad dell on the landward side of the castle, and turning sharp left just beyond the upper end of the barbican. On the way, one sees the memorable panorama of the southern façade of the castle, in which the various periods of building can clearly be distinguished.

The steps lead up a grassy slope, and to the right a doorway, cut through the walls, leads into the town car park. The infirm, or those short of time, may prefer to drive to this car park. Turning left from the doorway, at the f eastern end of the car park, there is a magnificent view of the castle across the intervening dell.

Near this point, the town walls now end i a small square tower, but originally a thinne wall crossed the castle ditch to link up with the walls of the castle itself. Some traces of them are still visible near the point of junction.

Along the line of the wall was a series of t semi-circular towers with open backs. These towers had no internal floors or arrowslits and could only have been defended from the wall-walk. There were two between the cast ditch and the town gate, though the one nearest to the latter is now much reduced i height. The wall here was recently breached to provide access to the car park.

In medieval times the town gate at Chepstow was the only entry into the town from the landward side. It was originally built by Roger Bigod III but was much rebuilt and altered in the later Middle Ages. The windows are nineteenth-century alterations.

The town gate was until recent years the only entry into Chepstow from the west and it still spans the main road into the centre of the town. A tall, rectangular tower with a single room above the archway, it may date back to the time of Roger Bigod, but it is much rebuilt and altered. In its present form is basically late medieval with nineteenth-century window openings and patching. It may have been largely rebuilt in the fifteenth century, if it was the 'New Gate' mentioned in 1487 and it was again rebuilt by the earl of Worcester as a prison in 1524. The two draped shields, now much worn, on its outer face date from one or other of these rebuildings.

On the other side of the town gate, the wall can be picked up again behind the Royal George Hotel and beyond the recent breach for the inner relief road, it is at its best as it rises up the slope, with another well-preserved tower mid way along its length. It survives to wall-walk level, with much of the parapet. The horizontal line of holes at the base of the latter were for drainage. The wall is built directly off the limestone rock and there is no ditch in front of it.

At the top of the slope, beyond the breach giving access to the school, its outer face, with two further towers, becomes obscured by modern houses and gardens. It ends on the bluff at the bottom of Green Street. On the lower flat ground beyond this, the wall, originally breached in the nineteenth century for the railway, was totally removed in the 1914-1918 war to provide additional space for a shipyard. The destroyed stretch included three of the towers. The final surviving stretch can also be seen from the inside near the railway station, though here the ground behind the wall has been quarried away so that its rear face now stands above a cliff-like rock face instead of the original slope.

Though sadly mutilated by what were seen locally at the time as the needs of the town, the surviving parts of Chepstow's town wall have a dignity and an interest which makes a walk along them well worth while. There is little direct architectural evidence for their date in the form of dressed stonework, but they are very similar to other town walls of the time of Edward I, not least those in his castle towns of north Wales. The work of Chepstow may date to about 1272-78.

The town walls, built in the time of Roger Bigod III remained intact until the present century. This well-preserved section lies south of the town centre, beyond the main inner relief road.

Runston Church

The Medieval Background

T HE SITE OF THE DESERTED VILLAGE of Runston stands on a low hill or plateau of Oolitic limestone some three miles (4.8km) west of Chepstow, and just to the north of the Chepstow-Newport road. The village was essentially a product of the Anglo-Norman settlement in Gwent Is-Coed (Gwent 'below the wood south of the Wentwood ridge), following the establishment of Chepstow Castle in th late eleventh century. The ruins of the twelfth-century Norman church are in the ca of Cadw, but the remains of the village are on private land and there is no public access.

There are many villages and small settlements in the southern Welsh coastal plain, whose names combine that of their original Norman owners with the suffix -ton, a farm or settlement. Hence, there is Gileston — 'Giles's Farm', or Bishton — 'the bishop's (of Llandaff) manor'; this latter example replacing the original Welsh name, Llancadwaladr, which may have been difficult for the tongues of English settlers. Runston, which in a document of 1245 was *Runestun*

and *Ryngeston* in one of 1262, was presumably the farm or settlement of a cert. man with a name like *Rhun* or *Runa*. We do not know who he was, but he or his success would have been responsible for building th village church, at a time when manorial lor through much of Britain were building new parish churches in stone, supported by tithe and burial and baptismal offerings of their tenants. The dedication is to St Keyna, probably the patron of Keynsham in Somerset, and of whom the lord of Runston had perhaps obtained a relic.

Runston church from the south-west. At one stage there was a towe the west end, later replaced by a bellcote which survives to gable height.

A Description of the Church

THE CHURCH CONSISTS of a simple rectangular nave and square chancel, and is very similar to other small Anglo-Norman churches in the area, such as nearby Portskewett. There was at one stage a square west tower, but this was later demolished and replaced by a bellcote. Only the foundations of the tower, found during conservation work, now remain. Nave and chancel stand largely intact to full gable height, lacking only the roof. They are built of locally quarried

The chancel arch, with its good-quality ashlar jambs and rounded arch.

Ground Plan of Runston Church

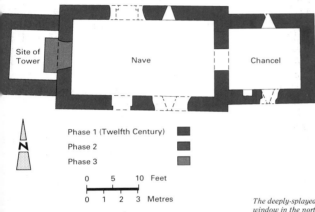

Site of Tower

Nave

Chancel

Phase 1 (Twelfth Century)
Phase 2
Phase 3

N

0   5   10 Feet
0   1   2   3 Metres

The deeply-splayed window in the north wall of the nave.

limestone, the walls of coursed rubble, with squared blocks of good quality dressed ashlar used for quoins, door and window openings, and the chancel arch. Many of the small square putlog holes into which the wooden scaffolding used to build the church was slotted can still be seen. Some of the ashlar has been robbed for farm buildings and the like, so that some door and window openings are now ruined.

The chancel was lit by a pair of splayed round-headed windows in its north and south walls, though that on the south is now ruinous. There would have been a third window in the centre of the east wall, but this vanished in later rebuilding of the masonry. There is a small recess, probably for a *piscina* (a holy water stoup), in the south wall. The chancel arch remains intact, with masonry jambs, and plain chamfered imposts and a round-headed arch, all in good-quality ashlar.

The nave had a pair of round-headed windows like those in the chancel, the northern example still surviving intact. There were north and south doors, again in round-headed openings, now largely robbed of their dressed stonework. When complete, these would have been similar to the chancel arch, but each may have had a tympanum — a stone panel, possibly decorated, filling the semi-circular space between door and arch.

On the west end of the church, the foundations of the tower can be seen, built against the earliest Norman masonry and clearly later in date. At some period the tower was abandoned and a large buttress built to support a bellcote. A fourteenth-century font, now in the National Museum of Wales, is thought to be from the church; a medieval grave cover lies just outside the south side of the nave.

The Decline and Abandonment of the Village and Church

S OME TWENTY FIVE house sites, including a possible manor house complex, are visible around the church and these probably represent the expansion of the village to its maximum extent. In the later Middle Ages, the population of Britain was falling due to climatic decline and pestilence, and many settlements on poorer marginal land declined. In this, Runston was no exception. By the middle of the sixteenth century a survey suggests that there were no more than nine houses still occupied (and perhaps less). The church remained in use for burials into the eighteenth century, the last body being laid to rest about 1770. By 1772 the number of houses was down to six. According to two Victorian antiquaries, 'the cottages which formed the village were purposely allowed to fall to the ground, as the best way of dislodging the inhabitants who were a most lawless and troublesome set of people, subsisting by smuggling, sheep stealing, poaching and other predatory acts . . .'. We should, none the less, bear in mind that forest edge communities like Runston had, historically, a long tradition of independence of mind in matters such as

firewood, rabbits and small game, and this w
not always appreciated by landlords and gamekeepers (both antiquaries were county landowners).

However exaggerated the reports of such lawlessness (the eighteenth century, after all had other methods of dealing with sheep stealing), it is all too likely that the landowners — the Lewis family of St Pierre and Penhow — did all they could to encourage the tenants to leave by allowing the houses to fall into ruin. Runston had in any case always been a poor and marginal village and there were new jobs to hand in th developing port of Newport, and in the new towns of industrial Gwent. By the time Archdeacon William Coxe visited Runston in 1798 (in moonlight, in the romantic tradition), the site — including the church – had become an archaeological site.

The church stands near the north-western edge of the former medieval village, now represented by no more than a series of earthworks.

Ground Plan of the Deserted Village of Runston

(After Caple, Jarvis and Webster) Note: There is no Public Access to the Village Earthworks

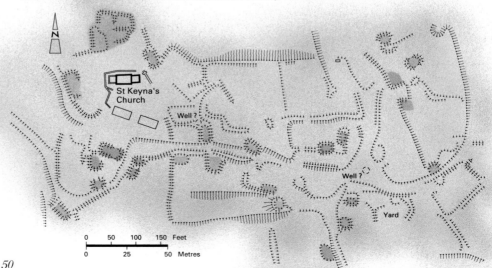

Chepstow Bulwarks Camp

BULWARKS CAMP is a small promontory fort of the pre-Roman Iron Age, overlooking the River Wye, here a tidal water, near its confluence with the Severn. On the river side of the camp, Hardwick Cliffs, some 170 feet (52m) high, are a formidable defence. To the south is a natural slope. The western and northern sides, which lack natural defence, are protected by a substantial bivallate (double) earthen rampart, with a main inner bank and a lesser outer bank. The inner bank has hints of a drystone revetment on its outer face, visible where the bank is eroded. The area enclosed within the camp defences is somewhat less than 2.5 acres (1ha).

The site has never been explored by archaeological excavation, and nothing is known of its history. It is, however, one of a series of hillforts and defended enclosures situated throughout south-east Wales which must represent the late Iron Age tribe of the *Silures,* who gave the legions so much trouble in the period AD 50-75. The hillforts, with their often massive banked and ditched earthwork defences are probably some centuries older than this. They may well represent the defended seats of tribal notables or chieftains, perhaps akin to the equites or knights whom Julius Caesar recorded as playing a leading role in the somewhat similar tribal society of Gaul. These pre-Roman forts tend to fall into two broad groups: the smaller examples as here at Chepstow, and the much larger sites — the true hillforts — with greater enclosed areas and more massive defences. It would, though, be difficult to say whether this division represents some form of ranking or social stratification among the tribal lords.

Whatever their ranking, these forts represent, as we know from excavation of similar sites, communities of people living in circular timber houses and practising a mixed agricultural ecomomy, growing wheat and barley (the latter for brewing as well as for bread) and with cattle and other domestic livestock. Their economy supported craftsmen (and women) such as potters, weavers and blacksmiths. The inhabitants also traded further afield for some necessities such as containers of salt which could not be obtained locally.

Plan of Bulwarks Camp

Playing Field

Alpha Road

Hardwick Cliffs

River Wye

0   150   300   Feet

0   50   100   Metres

The ramparts at the site are today much overgrown and disguised by tree cover.

Today, the ramparts at Bulwarks Camp are wooded and much overgrown, whilst the interior of the site is leased to the local authority for use as a football field and play area. Two larger hillforts can be visited nearby at Llanmelin (in the care of Cadw) above Caerwent, and at Sudbrook Camp near Portskewett.

Castell Cas-gwent: Crynodeb

S aif Castell Cas-gwent ar grib greigiog uwchlaw aber Afon Gwy yn y gwarchod prif lwybr yr arfordir o Loegr i Gymru. Ei hen neuadd a adeiladwyd o fewn pum mlynedd i Frwydr Hastings, yw'r adeilad seciwlar hynaf y ceir sicrwydd ynglŷn â'r dyddiad ac a godwyd o gerrig ym Mhrydain. Gan William fitz Osbern, arglwydd Breteuil yn Calvados y cafodd ei adeiladu ac mae'n debyg iawn i neuaddau'r unfed ganrif ar ddeg yn Llydaw a dyffryn Loire. Mae'r castell cynnar hwn yn arbennig hefyd oherwydd y ddau feili cerrig a saif bob ochr iddo. Yn arferol amddiffynfeydd pren oedd yn y cestyll cynnar.

Tua 1200 O.C. adeiladwyd wyneb dwyreiniol y castell gan William Marshall yr hynaf, un o filwyr amlycaf ei ddydd. Fe'i codwyd yn unol â'r dull amddiffyn newydd sef tyrau crwn yn ymwthio allan o'r llenfur i'r gwŷr bwa gael cyfle i gadw llygad ar y tir o'u blaenau. Cas-gwent yw un o'r enghreifftiau cynharaf ym Mhrydain o'r dechneg filwrol hon. Yna fe ehangwyd y castell a'i atgyfnerthu gan bum mab William Marshall a buasai pob un ohonynt farw erbyn 1245. Hwy a fu'n gyfrifol am adeiladu y tŷ porth allanol yr eir trwyddo heddiw i'r castell ynghyd â'r ward allanol y tu ôl iddo ac a ychwanegwyd y tu allan i'r castell cynharach. Gwnaethant hefyd ehangu gwrthdwr neuadd William fitz Osbern gan ychwanegu barbican amddiffynnol ym mhen ucha'r castell. Ar ddiwedd y drydedd ganrif ar ddeg, yn ystod teyrnasiad Edward I, fe wnaeth Roger Bigod III, un o wŷr grymusaf y deyrnas adeiladu neuadd helaeth a chymhleth ar gyfer ei nifer mawr o ddilynwyr. Ychwanegodd hefyd dŵr mawr yn ongl y ward allanol (Tŵr Marten) a gynhwysai ystafelloedd a chapel preifat.

Nid ychwanegwyd unrhyw adeiladau o bwys at y castell wedi hynny er i nifer o wahanol newidiadau domestig, yn cynnwys ffenestri helaeth, gael eu gwneud yno yn yr unfed ganrif ar bymtheg. Adeg y Rhyfel Cartref delid Cas-gwent gan wŷr y brenin ac er y brwydo a fu yn yr ardal, yn dilyn gwarchae byr ym mis Hydref 1645 gan ŵr lleol, Syr Nicholas Kemeys ynghyd â charfan o wŷr lleol a oedd yn parhau'n deyrngar i'r brenin. Gan Cromwell ei hun y dechreuwyd y gwarchae, yna trosglwyddwyd yr awenau i'r Cyrnol Ewer na fu ei wŷr yn hir cyn torri trwy'r amddiffynfeydd. Saethwyd Nicholas Kemeys. Cadwyd milwyr yng Nghas-gwent hyd 1690 pan aed â'r gynnau oddi yno i Iwerddon. I'r cyfnod diweddaraf hwn hefyd y perthyn y dolenni

cynnal gynnau ar y canllawiau. Tua'r un adeg fe ddefnyddid y castell i gadw carcharorion gwleidyddol. Yn eu plith yr oedd yr Esgob Jeremy Taylor, awdur *Holy Living* a *Holy Dying* a garcharwyd gan Cromwell ynghyd â Henry Marten, Gweriniaethwyr asgell chwith, ac un o'r gwŷr a lofnododd warant marwolaeth Siarl I. Treuliodd Marten flynyddoedd lawer yn y tŵr a does ryfedd iddo gael ei enwi'n Dwr Marten.

Drwy'r tŷ-porth allanol yr eir i'r castell heddiw. I'r de y mae bloc neuadd Roger Bigod lle ceid trefniadaeth gymhleth i baratoi a chyflwyno bwyd i'r neuadd. Ceir yma hefyd seler helaeth fwaog. Ar yr ochr gyferbyn y mae Tŵr Henry Marten. O'u blaenau y mae'r ddau dŵr crwn a gawsai eu hychwanegu at wyneb allanol y castell fel yr oedd pethau'r pryd hynny gan William Marshall yr hynaf. Drwy fynd drwy'r ward ganol, daw'r ymwelydd i floc neuadd cynnar William fitz Osbern. Ar y llawr cyntaf yr oedd y neuadd yr eir iddi ar hyd grisiau yn nyfnder y mur ac a godai fin y drws pen-grwn. Gellir yn ddigon rhwydd wahaniaethu rhwng ffenestri pen-grwn y gwaith gwreiddiol a bwâu pigfain y newidiadau diweddarach.

Unwaith fe geid yn nhŵr sgwâr y beili uchaf ystafelloedd byw hyfryd iawn ar gyfer yr iarlles o bosibl. Ar ôl croesi'r bont deuir at y barbican a ychwanegwyd gan feibion William Marshall i amddiffyn y pen hwn o'r castell.

Further Reading

Chepstow Castle
R.A. Brown, *English Castles*, 3rd ed (London 1976).
D. Crouch, *William Marshal: Court, Career and Chivalry in the Angevin Empire 1147-1219* (London 1990).
P. Gaunt, *A Nation Under Siege: The Civil War in Wales 1642-48* (London 1991).
J.C. Perks, *Chepstow Castle*, 2nd ed (HMSO, London 1967).
C. Platt, *The Castle in Medieval England and Wales* (London 1982).
D.M. Robinson and R. Thomas, *Wales: Castles and Historic Places* (Cardiff 1990).

Runston Church
R. Caple, P.H. Jarvis and P.V. Webster, 'The Deserted Village of Runston, Gwent: A Field Survey', *Bulletin of the Board of Celtic Studies*, **27** (1976-78), 638-52.
O. Morgan and T. Wakeman, *Notes on the Ecclesiastical Remains at Runston, Sudbrook, Dinham and Llan-bedr,* (Monmouthshire and Caerleon Antiquarian Association 1858).